STARTING A PART-TIME FOOD BUSINESS

EVERYTHING YOU NEED TO KNOW TO

TURN YOUR LOVE FOR FOOD INTO A

SUCCESSFUL BUSINESS WITHOUT

NECESSARILY QUITTING YOUR DAY JOB

JENNIFER LEWIS

COPYRIGHT © 2011 BY JENNIFER LEWIS

PUBLISHED BY RABBIT RANCH PUBLISHING

ISBN 13: 978-0615437644

ISBN 10: 0615437648

COVER DESIGN MICHELLE DRAEGER

My deepest thanks to the food entrepreneurs mentioned in these pages

– and others – without whom neither this book nor my own business

would have survived all the ups and downs;

To Bryan for always listening when I say "So...I have an idea...;"

And to my parents who always told me to reach for the cookies.

CONTENTS

FOOD IS PASSION

In 2003 I was working my way up the corporate ladder, doing everything I was supposed to in order to succeed. Yet I felt unfulfilled and, truthfully, bored out of my mind. My day-to-day corporate responsibilities no longer excited me and I desperately wanted to do something different. I burned through countless hours sitting in my cubicle staring at my computer but daydreaming about opening a bakery. I even had a name picked out and menu items drawn up for my imaginary bakery. Baking has always brought me a tremendous amount of satisfaction and I've always loved the art of creating something by hand that other people eat and enjoy.

The reality, however, was that opening up a bakery just wasn't an option. I didn't have the finances necessary to open and run a bakery and I didn't want to put my entire life on the line with a bank loan or run up credit card debt to fund my dream. I needed my current salary in order to make ends meet, so giving it all up wasn't something I was realistically able to do.

Or was there an alternative? It took a few years but I eventually realized that it was possible to work for someone else and work for myself at the same time. I knew it wouldn't be easy, but it would give me a creatively-fulfilling life while continuing to earn a steady paycheck. It was a way, in a sense, to try the bakery world without having to entirely give up my financial security.

Five years ago I started my specialty food company and am currently running it myself while simultaneously working for a nonprofit organization. Personally I feel this provides the best of both worlds. My business affords me the creativity that comes with making a specialty food product as well as the latitude to make important business decisions without having to go through multiple layers of red tape. I get to use my imagination on a daily basis when developing new products and flavor combinations. At the same time, my 'day job' helps me feel that I'm making a difference in an organization. I also like knowing that every two weeks I'll earn a paycheck so that sales fluctuations in my own food business won't leave me with plenty of cash one month and broke the next.

Whether you're slaving away in a cubicle while daydreaming of turning your mother's secret jam recipe into the next 'it' food or wish you could turn your flare for flan into a moneymaking venture that doesn't conflict with your stay-at-home parenting responsibilities, it's possible to start up and run a successful part-time food business. Best of all, a part-time food business doesn't mean you can't one day grow the business into a full-time job if you want. By taking it slowly and growing a strong and loyal customer base, your part-time food business can grow into whatever you want it to be when and if you're ready.

In the interest of full disclosure, I have both a culinary degree and an MBA but the fact that you may not have either shouldn't stand in the way of your food entrepreneur dreams. Many of the most successful food entrepreneurs – some of whom will be featured in these pages – didn't have formal culinary or business training before starting their businesses. This book will take you through the steps necessary – from testing your recipes to setting up a workable business plan to specific laws governing food businesses – to start and run a successful part-time food business.

A note about how this book is organized. Most business professionals will tell you to write a business plan prior to obtaining business licenses or trying to find a place to sell your product. However, it's impossible to build a strong and reliable business plan until you fully understand all the components that go into it. This book places the business plan section towards the end with the aim of taking you through all aspects that will go into the plan before you actually write it. You may find it useful though to start drafting notes as you go through each section of this book so that when it comes time to write the business plan you already have a working outline you can draw from. A recommended Business Startup Checklist is available on page 134.

BEFORE YOU LEAP

A passion for cooking and/or baking is important and it will get you far, but many people have an overly romantic picture of what running a food business entails. Do you envision yourself daintily putting flourishes onto cakes? Then also envision yourself hauling around 50lb bags of flour. Can you see yourself making the perfect roast chicken for customers? Now see yourself making 101 roast chickens and ask yourself if you're still excited about roasting chickens. Finally toss in the fact that a food career requires you to stand for hours on end, you'll be covered in various ingredients, and your hands will look like....well, like you work with your hands.

Cooking for money is much more physically draining then simply baking a batch of cookies at home. So before you head down this path, honestly ask yourself if you are up for the physical nature of this line of work. If things go well you will go home at night tired and aching and you'll likely build up all kinds of arm muscles you never knew you had.

On the flipside, starting up a part-time food business is the perfect way to see if this new path is the right one for you. It requires a relatively low financial investment and it gives you the opportunity to test out your ideas and recipes on real customers. It will also give you a chance to test yourself to see if the reality of kitchen work lives up to the fantasy you have in your head.

How They Got Their Start
Svedala Bakery

After a nation-wide search for 'fika' turned up empty-handed, Svedala Bakery was born. Claes Bavik, a Swedish national, and his wife Kristina, a US citizen, had recently returned to the United States after several years working abroad in Europe and were craving a taste of home. Specifically, they were searching for 'fika' which is a combination of treats that are eaten with coffee throughout the day. "In Sweden it would be considered an insult not to offer a guest coffee and at least one of the fika treats," Kristina explains.

After moving to Seattle, a city with a large Nordic population, Kristina and Claes combed the city in search of their favorite delicacies. Despite the fact that area stores sported Swedish flags and signs promised Swedish goods, what little they found could be classified, at best, as Danish. "It's a very different flavor combination from Swedish goods," Kristina says.

Disappointed by their search, they went online and what they found available in the US was nothing like they could get back in Sweden. With nowhere else to turn, they started trying to recreate their favorite treats in their home kitchen. The friends they shared their goodies with urged them to open up a Swedish bakery and they realized that they weren't the only ones who missed the flavors of home. Plus, the strong coffee culture of Seattle was reminiscent of the role coffee plays in Sweden so they believed their treats would be enjoyed by non-Swedes as well. It seemed like a good fit so they decided to open Svedala Bakery.

At the time neither Claes or Kristina felt comfortable giving up their full-time jobs as scientists so in addition to working and raising their three children, they spent hours and hours testing their recipes to try and find the right ingredient combinations. "In Sweden, fika is made up of seven traditional treats that are offered with coffee so we decided that our company would offer a minimum of seven items at any given time," remembers Kristina.

"We spent months fine-tuning these first seven recipes. Though all are based on classic Swedish dishes, raw ingredients like sugar and flour, even the fat content in butter, is different in the US than what is used in Sweden." Trained as scientists, Claes and Kristina literally set up experiments in their kitchen where they would alter one ingredient or one quantity at a time and judge the results. They tested so many recipes that their children actually got tired of eating treats!

While testing the recipes, Claes and Kristina actively searched for a place they could sell their goods. A storefront wouldn't work for them since in addition to the cost of setting it up, they would have to staff the store while they both worked their full-time jobs. Instead, they had recently read about the explosive growth of farmers markets and realized that this was a way to start their company in a cost-effective manner and without interfering with their jobs. During that time they also leased a commercial kitchen space that was used several days a week by another company that they were able to use on the remaining days.

In all of their planning, the one thing they hadn't counted on was that the farmers' markets started taking vendor applications in January which had long since passed. Locked out of every area market, it was by sheer happenstance that Claes learned from someone standing in line behind him at the business registration office that one market in the suburbs was still looking for vendors.

From their very first day at that market they were selling out of product. "It was beyond what we had anticipated especially since we weren't selling treats that were immediately recognizable to most Americans," Kristina says. "We were surprised by how well we did." Every week they would make more fika treats than the week before and every week they sold out. It got to the point that people would stop by the booth to pre-order items for pickup the following week.

As their first summer at the farmers' market came to a close, Claes and Kristina drove around to neighborhood cafes that fit with their company's focus on natural ingredients and offered to sell their products wholesale. One café took them up on it so after the farmers' market ended for the season they still had a weekly standing order that helped pay their kitchen rent. *Around that time they were also approached by the Swedish Cultural Center about selling their breads through the Center and, later, contracted with them to provide open-faced sandwiches for the Center's weekly meetings.*

In an effort to maximize sales, they also started up an online retail store through their company website. "I felt if you're going to have an online presence you might as well have an online store as well," says Kristina. Since their products and company were so unique, their site was able to quickly tap into the Swedish-American market with minimal online advertising. During the holidays they also emailed their loyal farmers' market customers offering them traditional Swedish holiday goodies which, in conjunction with their wholesale business, kept them busy through their first holiday season.

This combination of sales strategies had their business in the black in its first year and during the second year things got so busy Kristina left her full-time position to focus exclusively on the bakery. They also opened a storefront in Seattle's historic Pike's Place Market and continued to grow their wholesale business by adding new accounts while maintaining their strong customer base through the farmers markets.

Four years after starting though, tired of spending every summer and every holiday working around the clock, Kristina decided that the business was not worth the time she was missing out on with her children. Unfortunately the bakery's busiest periods coincided with her children's school vacations and she wanted to spend time with them in their last years before they left home. After significant soul-searching, Kristina and Claes sold Svedala Bakery to someone who promised to continue their mission of providing traditional Swedish delicacies handmade from only the highest quality natural ingredients. Looking back Kristina has no regrets, "I believe we created something that benefited our local community and in a small way we helped keep Swedish traditions alive here in the US."

It should go without saying that before you open up a part-time food business your recipes need to be well tested. Thankfully, for this step you'll likely have lots of willing test subjects in your family, friends, and coworkers. Block out a little time every week to make a batch or two of the recipe(s) you'd like to sell and ask your taste-testers to critique the various versions. Based on the feedback you get, make slight changes to your recipe and take it back to your tasting panel. During these testing sessions, be sure to also test the ingredients you use to determine how different ingredient brands may affect the taste, texture, and consistency of your product.

If your recipes are not already calibrated into weight measurement, use your testing time to switch your recipes from "cups" to "ounces." This not only helps when you start increasing the recipes to make larger quantities, but it also makes figuring out your cost for each product significantly easier (see page 81 for Product Cost Analysis information). Scales for weight measurement can be purchased from any kitchen supply store.

These testing sessions are also a great opportunity to determine whether your product has to be made from start to finish in the same day or whether it can be stored at different points in the process and finished at another time. 'Par-baking,' a process of partially baking or cooking your product and freezing it with the intention of finishing it at a later day or time, is a way to start your product one day and complete it another. If your product won't allow for true par-baking, you may still be able to freeze it in its finished state without compromising quality. For example, a little secret of wedding cakes is that they are often baked in advance, frozen, and then thawed and decorated a day or two before the big event. Before you get upset that customers are spending good money for frozen cake, there's solid reasoning behind it. A freshly baked wedding cake is very airy and light and can't stand up to the multiple layers and construction required for a traditional tiered cake.

Baking the cake in advance, freezing it, and then thawing it before the big day makes for a heavier and denser cake that is less likely to fall apart under its own weight. Knowing how much flexibility your product has through par baking or freezing means you could, for example, freeze ten loaves of bread and finish baking each individually right before you sell them.

You should also practice storing your finished products. Test the shelf life to see how long your products can be stored before going bad. Do your products need to be stored fresh or refrigerated? Do they need to be packaged in any special packaging to maintain freshness? Lastly, understand how your product responds to different types of ovens and to changes in the weather. Does the cold dry air of winter change the taste, cooking time, or storage requirements of your product as opposed to hot and humid summer weather? Knowing your product inside and out, and understanding all of its idiosyncrasies, will go a long way in helping you determine a sales strategy that will be successful.

Buying Ingredients

Depending on the size of your town or city, there may be stores in your area that cater to food professionals and with your business tax ID number you will be able to shop at those stores and take advantage of their wholesale prices with no sales tax. Another option is to open up a wholesale account with a food wholesaler like United Natural Foods, Incorporated (www.unfi.com). Companies like this will sell you ingredients in bulk sizes at wholesale prices. The only downside is that there is usually a minimum sales amount which may exceed what you need or what you want to spend at any one time. The easiest option for most part-time food entrepreneurs is to take advantage of membership warehouse stores like Costco® or Sam's Club® where you can buy items in bulk at reduced cost. A list of other places to purchase ingredients begins on page 130.

How They Got Their Start
Cakes By Look

Rhienn Davis may have baking in her blood given that her great grandparents, newly arrived at the time from Germany, started up and ran a successful German bakery in Pittsburgh in the early part of the 20th century. But Rhienn never actually considered baking as a career option. Instead, she studied zoology with the goal of becoming a veterinarian. To put herself through school she worked in radio and TV while simultaneously attending classes. Once she had her bachelors degree, the idea of seven more years of college and the accompanying tuition necessary to become a large animal vet no longer appealed to her. Since she already had work experience in media, she easily found herself a media sales job and started working full-time.

"I've always had a real creative side and a strong analytical side as well," Rhienn explains. "It's tough to find a career that can balance both of those." Her media sales job met her analytical needs but her career lacked the creativity she craved. To offset that she started baking cakes at home for friends and family as an artistic outlet for her creativity. "People started asking me to make their birthday cakes, then their wedding cakes. Then their friends would call and then their friends' friends started contacting me," Rhienn remembers.

Everyone Rhienn made a cake for raved about her flavor combinations and decorating ability and encouraged her to open up a shop but Rhienn figured it was simply a pipe dream. "I used to sit there and dream about starting a business that would allow me to bake all day," Rhienn says. But with a full-time job, a toddler, and a new baby at home, Rhienn literally did not have the time to open up a food business. Not to mention that with two young ones at home, daycare costs ate up a significant chunk of Rhienn's paycheck so she couldn't even contemplate putting money into starting up a business.

Rhienn's husband knew that his wife was incredibly gifted when it came to baking and believed that she could run a successful baking business. He had encouraged her for years to take the leap into part-time entrepreneurship so, for Rhienn's 30th birthday he paid for her business licenses, insurance, and put down the deposit on her shared commercial kitchen space. "I don't know if I really had any faith that this business would go anywhere," Rhienn says, "but I wanted to give it an honest try and figured it would be more interesting then simply being in media sales my entire life." Rhienn decided to focus exclusively on special occasion cakes and cupcakes because she felt that was the food medium that gave her the most options for creativity.

In addition to working 40+ hours a week at her media sales job and helping her husband take care of their two boys, Rhienn started down the road to opening up her company. She knew that the look of her company was important so she hired a graphic artist with whom she worked closely to design the company's logo. Though Rhienn personally loved the whimsical and somewhat satirical Cakes By Look logo the graphic artist designed, a friend who had extensive marketing experience told Rhienn that she needed to make the logo more "clean-cut." Rhienn took that advice under consideration but in the end went with the 'edgier' original logo as she felt it was more in line with her own personality. "I didn't want to create a staid and boring company that would simply have me making ribbons on cakes all day," Rhienn says. "I wanted a company that was fun."

Ironically, even though Rhienn was in media sales, she admits that she didn't know much about Internet marketing. She knew she needed a website that caught people's attention so she bought a Flash website that enabled her to put in pictures of her cakes and cupcakes. "I've heard time and time again that the site is what really hooks people," Rhienn says. "I'm glad I invested the time and money into the site." Rhienn also tried to put herself in the mind of her customers. "I thought that if I were looking for cupcakes how would I find someone to make them for me and that led me to put some ads on Google® and FaceBook®."

At first, most of Rhienn's business came through friends and friends of friends. Even though business wasn't booming yet, life *certainly wasn't easy. Rhienn worked her media job during the day and then baked in the commercial kitchen at night. This left her husband as the primary caretaker of their two boys during the evenings. "That was honestly the most stressed we've ever been," Rhienn says. "Those first few months almost broke the business and I did question whether it was all worth it."*

Then one day while Rhienn sat in her cubicle at her media sales job, she received a call from someone at Nordstrom's corporate office who wanted to place an order. "I just sat there stunned for a few minutes that someone who didn't have a connection to me actually found my company and wanted to place an order," Rhienn recalls. She did manage to collect herself enough to take the order and get the caller's information. Then, right as the call was coming to a close, the caller said that she wanted to pay with a credit card. Unfortunately, Rhienn didn't have a merchant account set up to take credit cards and asked the caller if it would be possible to pay by cash or check instead. The caller said she'd look into it and call Rhienn back.

The call never came. After hemming and hawing over a potential lost sale – her first "real" sale! – Rhienn finally called back only to find out that they'd placed an order with another company. Though she was obviously disappointed, Rhienn couriered over a dozen cupcakes and a gift certificate. "They loved it and they said they'd definitely use me in the future." After that business really started to take off.

Rhienn jokingly calls herself the 'Queen of Weird' because of the requests she gets from clients. She's designed cupcakes that looked like sushi and a Captain Underpants™ birthday cake just to name a few of her unique creations. "I believe that people who are looking for something untraditional are drawn to my company because of the image I project through the website and through the logo. It shows that my company is a little different from your ordinary 'red roses on white cake' baking company."

With about 97% of her business being wedding related, she has had her inevitable run-ins with the occasional bridezilla or parent-of bride/groomzilla. *"I think my imagery and brand tend to attract brides and grooms who are more laid back,"* Rhienn explains, *"and about 95% of my wedding business is really great people. The other 5% though...wow...."*

In fact, the second wedding cake Rhienn ever made turned out to include a nightmarish mother-of-the bride who tested all of Rhienn's resolve. Throughout the tasting and contract process it became obvious to Rhienn that the mother-of-the-bride, who apparently had taken out a line of credit on her home to fund the wedding, was in charge regardless of what the rest of the wedding party wanted. When Rhienn still hadn't received final payment the night before the wedding she contacted the bride's mother who literally had a full-blown meltdown and threatened Rhienn if the cake wasn't delivered as promised.

Despite her better judgment but not wanting to punish the bride for the mother's inability to abide by the payment terms of the contract, Rhienn delivered the cake only to later have the mother-of-the-bride argue that Rhienn hadn't met all of the points in the contract to try and avoid paying Rhienn at all. It got so bad that Rhienn had a lawyer-friend draft a very strongly worded letter stating that if payment was not received then the next stop would be small claims court. The letter did the trick and Rhienn says that in hindsight it was good learning experience early on in her food career. *"It taught me that when it comes to special events you need to have a very detailed contract and make sure that definite boundaries are set. Before, I would allow people wiggle room but that experience jaded me and if I don't receive your final payment 15 days before your event you can bet you'll be getting a call from me by day's end."*

Dealing with a few stressed wedding participants may be one thing, but dealing with the government can be another one of those nightmares that has you pulling out your hair. In 2009 Rhienn's business had grown so much she hired additional part-time help which required that she file quarterly employment taxes which she did faithfully every three months. One day she received seven notices from the IRS all claiming that she owed back taxes – and penalties – for employees she had in 2008 and early 2009. *"I had to spend half a day getting affidavits which explained that I didn't have employees at the time and that it was a clerical error on their part. Stuff like that can drive you insane but there's really nothing you can do about it. When it's your small business you have to deal with all the administrative headaches that in a full-time position you could pass off to someone else."*

Even though Rhienn does have part-time employees now, she's still working at her media sales job forty hours a week. She dreams about one day being able to focus on her company full time but she says that the idea of not having a steady paycheck to help cover daycare and other costs just makes her and her husband too nervous. *"That part is really hard,"* she admits, *"we talk a lot about how it will be much easier to take bigger risks with the business once my kids are older."*

In the meantime though her business is growing strong. She says that in the last year she's been surprised by how many people have either heard of her company or even tasted her cakes or cupcakes at someone's wedding or birthday. *"Word is getting around and everyone continues to be really positive so I know when the time is right we'll be able to take this business to the next level."*

THE RED TAPE:
BUSINESS LICENSES & HEALTH CODE CERTIFICATES

Even after your recipes have been perfected there are a number of logistical items you'll need to address before you can start selling your products. This section highlights some of the laws governing commercial food sales. Please note that this section covers the generic rules and that every state may have slightly different requirements. This book tries to provide a guideline of what you may encounter when setting up your business but it's best to consult with an attorney or small business administration official with specific questions about what exactly is required in your county and state.

> ### Getting Started Tip
> The Small Business Administration has one of the most comprehensive websites (www.sba.gov) about what is legally required to start a business. The site highlights exactly what forms are required by your state and local authorities based on your zip code. This book also has a list of business and health code licensing websites divided by state starting on page 135.

Registering Your Business

When starting your business there are four main steps you'll need to follow in order to get your business registered with the appropriate parties:

Deciding On Your Business Format

In the US there are several options available with regard to how your business will be classified by the government. Which option you decide upon will impact everything from the taxes your business will owe to the level of personal financial risk you face in starting the business. The complexities and tax implications behind the differing business structures cannot be adequately described in detail here so you should talk to your local small business administration office or consult with a lawyer before making a final decision.

- Sole Proprietorship - A Sole Proprietorship is one of the easiest business structures to set up. In this structure, a single owner and the business are considered one and the same in the eyes of the law. Aside from minimal paperwork necessary to set up this business structure, one of the biggest benefits of Sole Proprietorship is that the business' profits and losses are reported directly onto the owner's personal tax forms. The biggest downside however is that your personal finances, including your home or other assets, may be at risk if the business can't pay its debts or is named in a legal matter.

- Partnership - Similar to a Sole Proprietorship except with two or more people. In a Partnership each partner shares in the risks and rewards of the business based on their percentage ownership interest. A Partnership is also easy and inexpensive to setup and the partners report their respective share of the business' profits and losses on their personal taxes. However, just like a Sole Proprietorship, partners can also be held personally liable for any debts, losses, or court judgments.

- Limited Liability Company (LLC) – A Limited Liability Company, also known as an LLC, is a hybrid business structure that gives business owners the relative ease and flexibility of a Partnership with the personal liability protection of a corporation. In an LLC, the business' profits and losses flow through to the members (owners are called members in an LLC) and can be divided according to each member's percentage of ownership in the company. While LLCs are slightly more complex to setup then Partnerships, the fact that LLCs protect the members personally from business debts and lawsuits is an important consideration. Setting up your business as an LLC is now an option in every state although each state does have slightly different requirements as to whether you need to draft and file Articles of Organization and/or an Operating Agreement. Since laws are different in each state, you should be sure to understand exactly what is required in your state before proceeding to set up an LLC.

- Subchapter S Corporation - Subchapter S Corporations, also commonly known as Sub S or S Corporations, are a specific type of corporate business structure that mainly governs the disbursement of business profits and losses to the shareholders (owners are called shareholders in Subchapter S Corporations). Anyone considering classifying their business as a Subchapter S Corporation should definitely consult an attorney to help them through the many rules governing this type of business structure. At a very high level, profits and losses from a Subchapter S Corporation flow to the shareholders who then report it on their personal taxes. This means that the business is taxed only once – on an individual shareholder level – rather than being taxed at both the corporate and on an individual level.

However, your business has to meet several criteria such as, for example, all shareholders must be US citizens to be eligible to be a Subchapter S Corporation. Another thing to note, which may be of concern to a part-time business just starting out, is that all employees of a Subchapter S Corporation – including a shareholder who also works as an employee – must be paid a "reasonable wage" for their work. This means that if you plan to work in the kitchen to create your food products and you want your company to be registered as a Subchapter S then you will then need to set up payroll for any employees even if you are the only one, pay all employees a "reasonable wage," and file the employment taxes your business will owe the government. While paying yourself a "reasonable wage" is a wonderful concept, when you're just starting out and are concerned about the cash flow of your business, the drawing of your own salary and the paying of employment taxes out of that cash flow may not make this business structure your best option.

- Subchapter C Corporation - Also known as C Corps or Chapter Cs, this business structure faces much more stringent government oversight and regulatory requirements. Anyone considering starting up a Subchapter C Corporation should consult an experienced attorney as the rules surrounding this business structure go far beyond what can adequately be covered here. In brief, the taxation rules around Subchapter C Corporations are such that any profits and losses are taxed on both a corporate level (paid by the business) and then again at the individual level as each shareholder must pay tax on the money they earn from the company.

Changing Business Structures

Many small, independently run businesses initially register as Sole Proprietorships, Partnerships, or LLCs. These are generally much simpler business formats and require less tax preparation. While you should give considerable thought to your initial business structure, the good news is that, with few exceptions, you can change your business structure down the road if you decide it's necessary or if your business grows in such a way that it would be beneficial.

Regardless, how you structure your business impacts everything from what taxes you and your business need to pay, to laws governing how your business must operate and can impact your financing options. As such, it is recommended that you speak with an attorney, small business administration representative, or other knowledgeable resource for guidance should you have any questions or concerns about the right business structure for your company.

Registering Your Business Name

Depending on your state and business structure, the name you register your company under may be as simple as your own personal name, the names of the partners, or a fictitious 'trade' name such as Joe's Baloney. Each state has a separate set of rules and may require that a name be registered with your state's Secretary of State and/or Department of Licensing. While it may sound complicated, don't be deterred. Every state has an online site that explains their specific steps and in most cases you should be able to complete the entire process online. More information, outlined by state, is available in Appendix XII on page 135.

Naming Your Business Tip

If you are registering a trade name for the business, keep in mind not just where the company is today but where you might like it to go in the future and avoid using a name that will lock you into one niche market. For example, rather than registering your company under the trade name 'Scrumptious Cookies,' register it as 'Scrumptious Baked Goods' or simply 'Scrumptious.' Even if you only currently plan to offer cookies, you will have the flexibility to grow into other areas such as croissants and cakes down the road if you choose to or if market demand changes. Give yourself room to grow with a name that can grow with you.

Trademarking Your Business Name

Though you certainly don't need to trademark your business name, it is worthwhile to look into the process and decide if you have the time and money to invest into trademarking the name you will use in any marketing, advertising, and packaging. Trademarking your business name will protect a competitor from using a similar business name that may cause confusion among your customers. As an example, Greta's

Gluten-Free Goodies wouldn't want a competitor to come into their same market with the name Gertle's Gluten-Free Goodies. The similarities between the two could easily cause confusion and Greta's customers may mistakenly buy Gertle's products resulting in a loss of revenue for Greta. By trademarking the name Greta's Gluten-Free Goodies, Greta could take action against Gertle in this instance and, if the Patent and Trademark Office ruled in Greta's favor, could force Gertle to change their business name. More information about trademarking your business name, logo, or other distinguishing mark can be found at the US Patent and Trademark Office's website (www.uspto.gov) or by consulting an experienced trademark attorney.

Obtaining Your Employer Identification Number

Even if you don't plan to hire employees, depending on the business structure you choose, you may need to register your business with the IRS and obtain your Employer Identification Number (commonly referred to as an EIN). The IRS website (www.irs.gov) has a comprehensive guide outlining who needs EINs and how to obtain them along with an online EIN application.

Register with Your State, County, and City

Depending on your local regulations, you may be required to register your business with your state and local tax authorities. During this step you will be given information about how to apply for a reseller certificate if it is required in your state. This certifies that you are a recognized business in your state and enables you to avoid paying sales tax on many of the ingredients you'll be buying for your business as long as the ingredients are going into products that will be sold to the public. As with other registration paperwork, most if not all of the state and local-level registration forms are available online in conjunction with extensive information about other requirements specific to your area.

Liability Insurance

While not required by the state or federal government, it's a good idea to get liability insurance for your company that protects against loss of sales or property in the event of a catastrophe and protects the business financially from lawsuits. Given how litigious our society has become, liability insurance provides you and your business with an added layer of protection from any lawsuits that may arise. This is especially important in the case of businesses that are structured as Sole Proprietorships or Partnerships where lawsuits could impact both your business and personal finances. Many larger, well-respected insurance companies offer small business liability insurance so ask your personal insurance agent for quotes or for references to other insurance companies who work with small businesses. While it can be an added expense when starting up the business, for a few hundred dollars a year liability insurance can provide you with $1,000,000 or more of liability coverage and the comfort that your business and your personal finances will be safe should someone file a lawsuit against your company.

Finding Your Kitchen

For food businesses, registering your company and getting your business licenses is just the beginning. In most states, if you want to sell your food products, your business will have to be permitted by one or more health departments. These laws are in place to ensure that all food items are made in kitchens that meet the sanitary requirements set down by the state to protect the public from food-borne diseases. A number of states have passed Cottage Food Laws which enable small food businesses that meet specific requirements to work from home kitchens. More information about home-based food business regulations, divided by state, can be found online at www.smallfoodbiz.com/home-based-food-business. If your business or your state does not allow you to use a home-based food business, you'll likely need to find a commercial kitchen to work out of. Don't worry, it's not as difficult as you may think. Several places that work well for a part-time food entrepreneur include:

[35]

Shared Commercial Kitchen Space/Kitchen Incubator

In the past five years or so, a new concept of "shared" kitchen space, or kitchen incubators, has popped up. While still found mostly in larger cities, the idea is that one individual or investor rents or owns the commercial kitchen space and then subleases the space to several food entrepreneurs on an hourly or monthly basis. This means that you only have to pay for the time you anticipate using which is significantly cheaper then leasing an entire commercial kitchen of your own. In many cases the shared kitchens will require you to schedule your hours in advance to ensure there aren't time conflicts with other entrepreneurs. For part-time food entrepreneurs the benefit is that you can work your kitchen schedule around the rest of your life and responsibilities. To find a shared commercial kitchen in your area, start by checking the commercial rental section of Craigslist® or other community forums.

Extra Time in a Neighborhood Restaurant or Bakery

Bakeries and restaurants that already have kitchen space may only use it certain hours during the day but they are still paying rent for a full 24 hours every day. Approach those establishments to see whether they'd be willing to rent you any of their 'off' time. Of course, keep in mind your schedule before talking to specific businesses. If you have to be home every day to take care of your children, talking to a restaurant whose 'off' hours conflict with the time you need to be home with the kids won't work unless you are willing to hire a babysitter.

Community Kitchen Space

The easiest space to find may be a community kitchen space such as at a church, synagogue, or other community association that puts on events or feeds large numbers of people. If these kitchens are only used sporadically or only used on specific days of the week, they may be willing to rent out times to you as an additional revenue source. Take stock of the equipment they have to make sure it includes everything you need and be sure to take into consideration any limitations this type of space may put on you. For example, if you want to open up a wedding cake business, a church's kitchen – which is typically busy on Saturdays and Sundays – may be occupied on the days you'd need it most. Along those same lines, a synagogue may not allow your meat jerky business into their kitchen due to dietary restrictions of their congregation.

If none of the above options work for you, ask other food entrepreneurs at farmers' markets or festivals to see where they do their cooking and if there's availability in those spaces.

Other Health Code Considerations

Before you sign a lease or rental agreement with a kitchen, make sure it meets your local health standards. In most cases, such as a shared commercial kitchen or existing restaurant or bakery, the spaces should already have their health inspection certification. If you are at all concerned, contact your local health department and see if they can come by to make sure the kitchen meets all the necessary standards. The last thing you want is to sign a lease only to realize that the kitchen doesn't have the required three-basin sink or other large piece of equipment the health department says you need before you can start selling your products.

Even if the kitchen is already approved by the health department, you will likely need to register your business with the health department and have a separate inspection done for your specific business. While it's always nerve-wracking when the health inspector comes by, they are simply making sure that you are following all the rules and, for instance, not storing an open container of powdered bleach directly above your flour. In most cases you will not be able to begin selling to the public until your health inspection is complete.

Information about health inspection rules is normally part of a food handler's certificate course that your state or county may require you to take. Contact your local health department for more information and, if necessary, specific class schedules. In most municipalities, the course is required for anyone who will be working with food or serving food to the public including wait staff. You will be required to have the certification as will anyone you employ who works with food. It is not uncommon for health inspectors to ask to see proof of your certification during health inspections so always have copies on file at your kitchen.

The idea that you have to find time in your busy schedule to take a safe food handling course probably made your groan. Turns out that most courses are only a few hours long and if you simply pay attention during the class and read the material they provide to you, the final test should be no problem. The benefit of this course is that it helps you and everyone who may work with you understand the risk of food-borne illness and how bacteria is spread through unsafe handling. If you pay attention to the class and put what you learn into action in your kitchen, you greatly reduce the risk of serving contaminated food. On the off chance that the thought of making your customers ill isn't enough to motivate you, then be aware that the health inspector may come by at any time to spot-check your business so always make sure your workspace is kept clean and conforms with all health codes.

Depending on what you are planning to sell or how you plan to sell it, you may also be required to be certified by the US Department of Agriculture (USDA) or your specific state's Department of Agriculture. For example, if you are selling your products wholesale or via your own online website you may need to register with your state's Department of Agriculture. Your local health department should be able to tell you if you need to register with either the state or federal Department of Agriculture prior to selling your products. Like health certifications and permits, a USDA or state Department of Agriculture certification may require an in-person visit by an inspector to ensure that you are following all applicable health code rules and you will likely be the subject of unannounced spot inspections in the future.

How They Got Their Start
Primal Pacs

A change in lifestyle combined with the economic downturn of 2008 was the driving force behind Matt Pierce starting up Primal Pacs. Several years earlier Matt and his wife were introduced to CrossFit®, a total body training program with gyms across the country. As they became more involved with CrossFit, they learned about eating according to the Paleo diet, a dietary lifestyle that encourages people to eat foods that haven't been altered by humans such as meat, vegetables and fruit, instead of foods that contain refined sugar, grains, and manufactured ingredients. Popular among CrossFit enthusiasts, a Paleo diet is seen as a way to eat a natural and balanced diet that will fuel an active lifestyle. "We tried to eat strictly Paleo for a while," Matt explains, "but we eventually migrated to an eating style that draws heavily from Paleo with a focus on eating as all-natural as possible but where we weren't penalized for enjoying a beer from time to time."

Matt's dad and uncle had been making their own homemade beef jerky for years so when Matt tasted a pre-packaged Paleo jerky product, he was unimpressed. "It wasn't as high quality as I knew beef jerky could be so I tapped into my family's expertise and started making beef jerky in my garage for my own use."

Around that same time the economy weakened and Matt, who had spent the previous 16 years in construction, found himself out of a job. "All the jobs just dried up," he remembers, "and I wasn't willing to look outside of the area for new work since my wife already had a solid job." Despite the fact that their income was effectively cut in half Matt felt that if there was ever a time to make a go of the jerky business it was now. "I spent years working in jobs I hated," he says. "I made good money but I didn't enjoy myself. I thought it was worth taking the financial hit to try and make something work that could be really cool." Luckily, Matt's wife, now the main wage earner in the household, agreed and encouraged Matt to take the leap into entrepreneurship.

Matt realized that his beef jerky made from quality ingredients had a built-in niche market with the segment of the population who are looking for all-natural healthy snacks. With that in mind, Matt went through about 80 iterations of his jerky recipe until he found the right jerky flavor made from premium grass-fed beef. Vacuum-sealed with fruits and nuts, the jerky also provides the right balance of natural sugars and fats which, along with the protein, makes for the perfect snack for people eating a Paleo diet and those who simply want something healthy to eat.

During the three months of recipe testing, Matt was giving his creations away to friends at his CrossFit gym and people wanted to know how they could buy the product so he officially registered his company. After finding commercial kitchen space at a kitchen incubator which he rented on an hourly basis, Matt began what has become an on-going and epic battle to get his business properly registered with the necessary health departments. "At first I approached my county health department," Matt explains, "but was told that since I made jerky I had to work with my state Department of Agriculture. But when I went to the state Department of Agriculture they sent me back to the county health department because apparently they don't deal with jerky products either. I went around and around until someone finally told me I needed to work with the US Department of Agriculture (USDA)."

As Matt has found out though, the USDA is not set up to work with small businesses. "The USDA is used to working with large corporations who have teams of lawyers and millions of dollars at their disposal. I honestly feel like every time I deal with the USDA they are trying to put me out of business." As just one example, Matt was required to send copies of his product label to the USDA Label Approval Office in Washington DC. Matt originally sent copies via fax, as is required, but six weeks passed and he hadn't heard back. Since the Label Approval Office doesn't provide companies with a phone number or email address for follow up, Matt went ahead and sent another set of labels via certified express mail. It took six more weeks to receive a response – only to find out that he needed to make changes to the label and start the entire process over again.

Thankfully, making the changes to the label itself wasn't nearly as stressful as getting it approved. Matt's graphic artist needed a new deck so Matt built that while she worked on his logo and label (and subsequent label changes) and though each were paid for their services, Matt essentially made as much on the deck as he paid for the graphics so there wasn't a huge impact to his finances. Matt also had a friend who was working to start up a web design business make his company's website. Since the friend needed to build up his work portfolio, he only charged Matt a nominal amount in exchange for being able to showcase the Primal Pacs site to potential clients. "At the end of the day I was able to get two crucial pieces of the business, the graphic design and the website, for next to nothing. That's critical when you're trying to start up a business on limited funds."

Without USDA approval, Matt is not currently selling his products to stores which is where he hopes to take his business in the future. He is still able to sell through his online retail store though and word has rapidly spread among other area CrossFit gyms. "I have a strong enough product that the business works solely through local sales," Matt says. "I have a great group of customers who are so loyal to my product that I have trouble keeping it in stock. The minute I make a new batch it flies out the door immediately."

While Matt still does small residential construction jobs for additional income, he has enjoyed the transition from the job site to the kitchen. Whereas some people complain about the physical nature of kitchen work to Matt the change is heavenly. "Construction is, obviously, a very labor intensive job. This past winter, when the weather was nasty, I couldn't get over how lucky I was to be inside and warm and not working knee-deep in mud and freezing my butt off outside."

Even though his business is growing, Matt is still somewhat tentative about his long-range plans for the business as he awaits final certification from the USDA. He has already received interest from a large national natural grocer whose buyer was introduced to the product through her CrossFit gym. Since both Matt and his wife love the outdoors, he likes that his company fits into that market as well and intends to talk to outdoor lifestyle stores about carrying his product for people who are looking for a healthy and portable snack for all their skiing, backpacking, kayaking, and rock climbing adventures.

Despite the trials and tribulations Matt has faced in starting up his company, he says he's glad he took the chance and started Primal Pacs. "Instead of pouring concrete I'm creating something that's good for people and offering them an all-natural healthy snack that's not chockfull of carbs and sugars like other processed snack options," he says. That doesn't mean Matt hasn't had his share of sleepless nights where he worries over finances or about what will happen if Primal Pacs doesn't work out. "Then the next morning I get in a bunch of new orders and the business just keeps growing," Matt says, "so I put the worrying on hold, put on my apron, and get to work."

SALES CHANNELS
WHERE YOU CAN SELL YOUR PRODUCTS

No matter how good your recipes are they aren't going to make you any money just sitting in your recipe box. What you want to know is where you can sell your products for profit. When people think 'food business' they usually mean a storefront, restaurant, or bakery. But those options are incredibly expensive to undertake and require you to be there full-time – usually 70+ hours a week. That is simply not an option for everyone. Thankfully in the past few years new options have emerged that make it easier to be a part-time food entrepreneur.

One thing you need to take into account is what you mean by 'part-time.' If you have a predictable work schedule or are a stay-at-home parent who has childcare on specific hours or days every week then you may be looking for something different then someone whose work schedule provides them with certain periods of the year that are slower, like teachers who have summers off. The type of 'part-time' business that fits with your life will guide you to a selling channel that works best for you.

Below is an explanation of different ways you can sell your product that are feasible on a part-time basis. These are by no means mutually exclusive. You may find that what works best for your specific product is a combination of two or more of these outlets. Just like the best recipes, a great business is usually developed by taking a pinch of this and a touch of that. As you read through the following section take into consideration your other time obligations to try and find a sales channel that will work for your product and for your life.

Wholesale

Selling wholesale is when you produce a product and sell it to a retailer who marks up the price and sells it to their customers. For example, let's say you make and bottle your grandfather's super secret BBQ sauce recipe and sell it to a local supermarket for $3.99 per bottle. The supermarket then puts it on their shelves and sells it to their customers for $5.99.

[43]

Benefits of Wholesale

- Wholesale orders are generally larger purchase amounts than you'd receive from an individual customer. While a customer may purchase one bottle of your BBQ sauce, the supermarket has to stock up so they may place an order for 36 bottles. You don't make as much money on every wholesale bottle but you can make up for it in the quantity you sell.

- For perishable items, such as baked goods, you will most likely have a standing order and a standing delivery day which enables you to plan it into your already busy schedule.

- Standing orders also mean that you have a certain amount of revenue that you can rely on week after week. This is different than when you sell directly to the public and don't know how much you'll make on any given week.

- By being sold through a retailer your product and your brand gain legitimacy more quickly. Customers assume that since said store carries your product it must be good and are more willing to give it a try. This may help you build customer loyalty more quickly and may also lead to future wholesale orders with other companies.

Downsides of Wholesale

- Since you sell your product at the lower wholesale price, you have to make sure that the quantity you're selling makes up for the decreased price since your product cost per unit remains the same. This can be accomplished by setting "case quantities" that stipulate that wholesale orders must contain a minimum number of units or that the wholesale order must exceed a certain minimum dollar amount.

- It's harder to build your brand since you don't interact with the customers directly. You are also at the whim of the retailer who may decide to put your product on sale and then your brand may start to be identified as a bargain-basement priced item which, if that's not the type of customer you want to attract, can detract from your brand image.

- Retailers may not make quick decisions. They may want to taste your product and then go away and think about it for awhile. Just when you start to lose all hope they may come back with several questions. Then maybe they'll ask for another tasting. If you're looking to make money from day one, wholesale may not necessarily be the way to go.

How To Get Wholesale Accounts

The key here is research, research, research. You need to know everything about your product, your competitors, and your customer segment (see Building A Business Plan starting on pg. 77 for more in-depth information). After you have all of that information you need to research which retailers your product would be a good fit for and why. What opportunity does your product offer for retailers? Perhaps your BBQ sauce is an authentic St. Louis style sauce and the retailers you've identified don't sell any St. Louis style sauces. Be prepared to explain to retailers the virtues of St. Louis style BBQ sauce and why carrying your sauce will increase their sales.

When you feel you have all that information, call up the retailers you've targeted and ask to speak to their buyer. If it's a larger retailer you may need to ask for the buyer for a specific department – like the condiments buyer for our BBQ sauce example. The buyer should be able to tell you their process for deciding on new products. In many cases they'll want to taste your product and during the tasting you can explain to them why your product will bring in more revenue for them. The first few times you meet with buyers may be nerve-wracking but with practice your sales pitch will become easy and natural.

Another way to get your products in front of food buyers is to attend a food tradeshow such as the NASFT Fancy Food Shows (www.specialtyfood.com). While significantly more costly than approaching buyers individually, the benefit here is that in one tradeshow you can get your product in front of possibly hundreds or even thousands of potential retailers, brokers, and distributors. While this may sound like a fabulous idea, keep a few things in mind before going this route.

Tradeshows can be incredibly expensive after you add in your booth fees which can be several thousand dollars, transportation, hotels (if necessary), the food samples you'll have to provide buyers, etc. You will want to do your homework and try to find a tradeshow that brings in the type of buyers you're looking for and that feature products like yours. Going back to our BBQ sauce example, you would hate to waste money going to a dessert tradeshow (yes, there is such a thing!) with your BBQ sauce because the buyers there wouldn't be interested in condiments. If possible, try to attend a tradeshow at least once before committing the money to attend it as a manufacturer so that you can see the type of buyers it attracts, how people set up their booths, and other logistics.

Before attending a tradeshow you should also keep in mind whether you can handle the type of quantity that may come out of the show based on your 'part-time' lifestyle. Let's say that your product is a huge hit at the show, can you handle the necessary production needs to make enough product for all the orders? Only consider attending a tradeshow if you can ramp up production considerably or have the flexibility to work significantly more hours if your product is a hit with buyers.

Things to Keep in Mind When Selling Wholesale

- Establish minimum case quantities that will enable you to make money on every order. Selling a single bottle of BBQ sauce at a wholesale price of $3.99 may not be worth your time and energy. But if you can sell the sauce in case quantities of 12 then every order is at least $47.88 which starts to look much more attractive.
- Packaging is key when it comes to wholesale orders. Since you aren't there to tell the end customer about your product's attributes – what makes your product good and different from every other similar product – your packaging has to speak for you. You may also need to have all ingredient and nutritional

[46]

information on your packaging. Contact your local health department for more information and then research and design packaging that will help showcase your product in the best possible light.

- Shelf life is critical to retailers as they want a product that can stay on their shelves without going bad. Make sure you've tested your product and can tell them exactly how long your product will be fresh and viable.
- Don't limit yourself to supermarkets or grocery stores. Many other types of retailers carry food products such as gift stores and lifestyle stores. Stores that cater to tourists may also be an option if your product has a strong regional connection.
- Before entering into any wholesale contracts take the following into account:
  o How are you getting paid? As long as the retailer is credit worthy, checks are the easiest method of payment and you won't have credit card processing fees taken out of the payment you receive. However, it's always advisable that you have retailers' credit card numbers so that you can charge their card if they don't pay on time.
  o When are you getting paid? Any contract you sign or purchase order you receive should describe when you will be paid – either on delivery, Net 15 (15 days after you ship or deliver the order), Net 30 (30 days after you ship or deliver the order), etc. It's important to know this so that you know when to expect your checks and build it into your anticipated cash flows accordingly. You don't want to be counting on Invoice #310 to help you pay your kitchen rent when that invoice isn't due to be paid until the 15th of the following month.
  o Can they return items to you? It should be outlined in the contract or purchase order whether retailers can return unsold product to you after a certain period of time.

Merchant Accounts Explained

A merchant account enables businesses to accept credit cards and debit cards in exchange for goods or services. In a nutshell, when a customer buys an item and pays for it with a credit or debit card, the business charges the card which alerts the merchant account. The merchant account acts as an intermediary between the business and the credit card issuing company. The merchant account credits the money to the business' account and then works with the credit card issuing company to, essentially, be reimbursed.

For in-person sales a credit card terminal is required. This is a physical credit card processing machine that you use to charge the customer's card. For online sales and e-commerce an internet payment gateway or virtual terminal is needed.

All merchant account companies charge fees for using their services which may include, among others, a monthly fee for the credit card terminal and/or access to the payment processing center, a set charge per transaction, and a percentage of the sale price. Some of these fees go straight to the merchant account while others are passed onto the specific credit card issuing companies themselves. These fees can start to add up quickly so shop around for the best rates and the best combination of services. An easy place to begin your search is with companies like PayPal® or Costco® who both offer merchant account services to small businesses as do Quicken® and QuickBooks® for those who use their accounting software programs. Don't forget that this is your business revenue so be sure you understand and are comfortable with all the terms of the merchant account you sign up with.

- What type of liability do they require you to carry? When it comes to food items, many retailers will require that you carry a specific amount of liability insurance and require that they be named as an additional insured on your insurance policy so that they are protected from lawsuits involving your products.
- How far in advance must they notify you of changes to a standing order? If you deliver 10 dozen cookies once a week to your local coffee shop, the last thing you'd want is for them to call you four hours before the scheduled delivery time to say they actually need 20 dozen this week. Build in a timeframe that works with your schedule for when they can and can't change standing orders.

- Lastly, don't get frustrated if you hear "No" a lot in the beginning. It's inevitable that not every buyer will be interested in your product and while it hurts to hear no, especially given that this is a product you've made with you own hands, it is not a commentary on you or your product. It may just mean that you've approached the wrong retailer and need to find one that is a better fit for your product.

Wholesale Startup Costs

After your initial startup fees, things like renting commercial kitchen space and getting the appropriate licenses, the cost to acquire wholesale accounts, outside of tradeshows, is negligible other then the cost of your time calling on the buyers, giving them samples of your products, and showing them examples of the packaging.

Farmers' Markets

Farmers' Markets are one of the easiest and least expensive ways for a new food business to start selling products. And with the current emphasis on 'eating local,' there seems to be new farmers' markets popping up everyday all around the country. In most cases, you will have to complete an application in order to participate in the market and, if accepted, will likely be required to commit to a specific number of weeks or timeframe. If the market is a seasonal market, they'll usually ask that you attend each week's market in that given season. If the market is year-round they may break the year up into 'seasons' and then ask that you attend on a weekly basis for your allotted season. Payment to the market other than possibly a small application fee when you apply to be part of the market, is usually a percentage of your sales at the end of market day. This means that how much you owe to the market association every week is dependent on how successful your product is with customers.

Benefits of Farmers' Markets

- Unlike wholesale accounts, at farmers' markets you interact directly with customers and sell your product directly to them. Therefore you sell at your retail price point and can capture the full profit.
- Farmers' Markets are a great way to test your product since you can get feedback from your customers immediately to determine if anything should be changed with your products. Also, if you plan to offer several different products or several different flavors, farmers markets can provide valuable and relatively inexpensive market research into what sells best and what is not as popular with customers.
- The face-to-face interaction between you and your customers at the farmers' markets helps you quickly build a loyal following so that if you do decide to pursue additional sales avenues in the future you already have a customer base that recognizes your brand.

- Most farmers' markets are cash-only. This means that you don't need to invest in a merchant account and you won't have to pay credit card fees on every sale.
- Since you will be assigned to attend a certain number of weeks and since the farmers markets occur on the same day or days every week, you will know in advance when you need to be at the market and can plan the rest of your schedule accordingly. This is especially helpful for part-time food entrepreneurs as you can apply only to markets that fit into your schedule.

Downsides of Farmers' Markets

- Farmers' Markets usually don't accept more then one or two of the same kind of vendors. This makes it harder for a new food entrepreneur to get in if that market already has a strong performer with similar products.
- You typically have to commit to a season's worth of weekly farmers' markets so, for example, you have to be willing to spend every Sunday between 8-2 during the summer selling your products. Make certain you want to and can commit to that type of time week in and week out, rain or shine.
- To make your selected space inviting to customers, you might have to provide a tent canopy, table, chairs, etc, in addition to what you plan to bring to sell. This means that you will have to set up and take down this display for every market which can get tiresome.
- Since your 'store' is essentially outdoors, even if it is covered with a tent canopy, weather can have a larger then normal impact on your sales. Chocolates may melt in summer months or customers may simply not want to buy ice cream on a cold and blustery day.
- The farmers' market association usually has a set minimum amount they require in weekly fees to help with the organization and logistics of putting on the event. You may be required to either pay a percentage of your sales or the

minimum amount depending on which is greater. Should you have a terrible day with no sales, you would still be required to pay the stated minimum fee.

How to Get Into a Farmers' Market

As part of your research, visit your area farmers' markets and decide which markets work best for your products. In addition to making sure that the market's day and time commitment work for you, consider the type of customer that comes to that market and whether or not there is a competitor for your product already selling at that market. After you've narrowed down your list, contact that market's association to request a copy of their application and rules. This is usually easily found online or by asking at the market's information booth. If there is no information booth, ask one of the market vendors who you should speak with. Depending on how far in advance of market season you contact them, the new application may not be ready in which case ask how you can be added to their vendor email list so that you can be alerted when the next season's application becomes available.

Things to Think About with Farmers' Markets

- Farmers' Markets try to focus on fresh and local items like fruits, vegetables, and local meats. As much as you possibly can, incorporating local and all-natural ingredients into your products improves your chances of being accepted into the farmers' market and the better your product will likely sell with customers. Be sure to tell customers if any ingredients in your product have been purchased from other farmers markets vendors.
- Market customers like to try food before they buy it so be prepared to give away samples of your product. The samples don't need to be giant; a simple bite should be enough for customers to decide whether or not they like the item enough to buy it.

- Make sure you know if you are required to charge sales tax. Since you are selling directly to the customer, your state, county, or city may require that you charge sales tax which they will then collect from you. Look into this in advance so that you don't end up paying any owed sales tax out of your own pocket.
- Before you start selling, know whether you are required to have ingredient and nutritional information on any product labels.
- Deal in whole numbers. Selling an item for $9.99 may sound catchy but then you'd better come to the market with lots of coins. Whenever possible, price your products in whole dollar amounts to make everyone's lives easier. On that same note, if you are required to charge sales tax, building it into the product's cost and making it a whole dollar amount is much less hassle for you and your customer. For example, charge the customer $5 for a product and back the sales tax out of it separately rather than telling the customer it's "$4.95 plus tax."
- Bring lots and lots of change! Customers seem to flock to farmers' markets straight from the ATM and are flush with $20 bills. Your product may only be $3 but you're still going to have to break lots of large bills. Make your life easier and come prepared with $1 and $5 bills for change.

Farmers' Market Startup Costs

Just like selling wholesale, your startup costs will initially include expenses like commercial kitchen space rent and business licenses. For farmers' markets your costs will also include any market application fee, booth decorations such as a tent canopy and table you may need to buy, signage (if permitted), as well as a percentage of your weekly sales that you'll need to pay to the farmers market association.

Craft Shows and Festivals

Craft shows and festivals are similar to farmers' markets in that you create a 'store' and sell your products directly to customers.

Benefits of Craft Shows and Festivals

- These are an excellent opportunity to test your products with customers without committing to a weekly farmers market schedule.
- Since you are selling directly to the public, you can charge the full retail price so that you maintain a healthy margin on your products.
- These events draw a wide range of customers so it's a great way to get your products and brand in front of numerous people.
- Since craft shows and festivals occur on pre-selected dates, you can apply to those that best suit your schedule and you'll know well in advance if you've been accepted.
- Customers at these types of events know that most vendors only accept cash, particularly for lower priced items, so you don't necessarily need to sign up for a merchant account.

Downsides to Craft Shows and Festivals

- Due to existing contracts with food manufacturers or facilities management, not every craft show or festival accepts outside food vendors.
- You will likely be required to pay for your booth space in advance. Fees may range anywhere from $25 for the event to $1000 or more so it can be an expensive proposition if you don't know how well your products will do in that environment.

How to Get Into Craft Shows and Festivals

After you've identified the shows and festivals you'd like to attend, you should be able to access the application through the organization's website or by contacting them directly. As much as possible, give yourself plenty of time in advance of the show deadline to read through the application and understand exactly what they need from you in terms of pictures or even tasting samples. Some of these events may be 'juried' which means that not everyone who applies is accepted into the event. As such, you will want to make sure that your application presents your company in the best possible light, including high quality photographs if photos are required in the application, to increase your chances of being accepted.

Things to Know about Craft Shows and Festivals

- Like farmers' markets, customers like to try food before they purchase it so be prepared to give away samples of your products. Just be sure to check the show rules carefully before doing so as some shows prohibit sampling.
- Again, like farmers' markets, know whether or not you need to charge sales tax for your products and, if so, build the tax into your selling price for convenience.
- Know if you need to have product labels that include ingredient and nutritional information.

- Try to deal in whole numbers when it comes to your sales price (and tax if applicable) so that making change is easier to facilitate.
- Bring lots of small bills with you to the event so that you can break $20 bills.

Startup Costs for Craft Shows and Festivals

After your initial business registration and licensing has been paid and you add in your kitchen rent expenses, the startup costs for craft shows and festivals will include your booth costs and, in some instances, show application fees. You will also need to spend money on obtaining things for your booth such as a table, chair, and any display items or signage.

Online Retail

Rather than incurring the expense of opening up a retail store and having to be present in the store every day, you can open up an online retail store to sell your products. While it sounds like a great idea from the outset, the reality is that selling food online is very tricky. Ask yourself this, when was the last time you purchased food online that you hadn't tasted before or that didn't come recommended either by a friend or sold through a catalogue? You can sell food online but without either a lot of marketing or a lot of luck, it's a hard road. However, in combination with other sales channels, this method will provide your loyal customers with another way to order from you and a way to order gifts for shipping.

Benefits of Online Retail

- A website is all that's needed to get up and running. While not inexpensive, it is nowhere near as expensive as opening up and running a retail store. If you want to lower your costs even further, rather than having a website created for your company, you can open up an Etsy® (www.etsy.com) or Foodzie® (www.foodzie.com) store which will enable you to sell through their site and you can direct your customers to the web address these web stores will provide.

- There's no weekly or seasonal commitment since you only have to bake or cook when you have an order.
- You can charge retail prices so you capture more of your products' margins.
- An online presence opens your company up to customers from different parts of the country.

Downsides of Online Retail

- It's hard to break through the online clutter and get noticed to get a sale. To be successful solely online without additional sales channels requires a strong marketing and advertising plan and the finances to back that plan up.
- There are people who illegally bake/cook out of their homes and sell online. Without any kitchen overhead, they can offer similar products at rock-bottom prices. If you choose to follow the rules and rent commercial kitchen space, your costs will naturally be higher which makes it hard to compete price-wise.
- While there's no weekly or special seasonal commitment, you will have to produce products when you get an order and that may not work if your schedule doesn't allow for much flexibility. For example, if you get an order on a Monday morning but can't produce the item until Saturday and then ship out the following Monday, the order is already a week old before it ships. In today's fast-paced internet sales world, it's hard to keep customers if you keep them waiting.
- You will need to use some type of merchant account service in order to sell online so that your customers can pay for their orders with credit cards. As mentioned previously, most merchant accounts charge a monthly fee – regardless of whether or not you have any sales that month – and also take a small percentage of every sale.

[57]

- Shipping can be problematic for some products and you'll need to investigate packaging and shipment options to see what combination will get your products safely into your customers' hands.

Things to Think About With Online Retail

- Depending on what you are selling you may be required to charge sales tax. Make sure that your website is able to automatically add this to the order total so that customers are automatically charged the appropriate amount of sales tax.
- Test how your product ships by sending it to friends around the country via different parcel carriers before offering it for sale online. Be aware of how changes in temperature may impact how well your product ships.
- A picture is worth a thousand words and when it comes to online sales this is especially true. The first impression customers will get of your products will be the pictures they see online so it is well worth it to hire a professional photographer to take product shots for you.
- If you are planning to focus on online retail sales, you'll want to make sure people can find your site. Ideally you want people to be able to put key search words into their search engine of choice and have your company website pop up as one of the top selections on the first results page. To help you with this process, known as search engine optimization or SEO, consult with an experienced web technician.

Startup Costs for Online Retail

There is really nothing stopping you from selling online. You can cheaply and easily set up your own Etsy, Foodzie, or other similar account or, if you're proficient at web design, your own website. Alternatively, you can contract with a web developer to design the site for you. A good web developer should be able to integrate an online shopping cart to your site so you can easily accept orders online. Other startup costs include your initial business registration and licensing fees, commercial kitchen rent, your monthly and per transaction merchant account fees, and any marketing costs.

Special Events

In our culture food is central to many of the special events we have throughout our lifetimes. Focusing your business on special events works particularly well if you have a product that is in demand for those types of events. The first food most people think of when it comes to special events is cake and it's possible for a baker to simply focus on wedding and celebration cakes and build a strong business. Even if you don't want to make cakes, there are other sales opportunities when it comes to special events such as packaging your product as favors for guests.

Benefits of Special Events

- Orders are usually placed well in advance so you can plan your schedule accordingly.
- You can accept or decline orders as you see fit depending on how they work with your schedule. If someone wants a cake delivered on a Wednesday afternoon but that's not a day you have childcare, you can simply decline the order and recommend them to another vendor.
- You charge retail prices so you can capture your full product margin.
- You can require that payment be made in either cash or check and avoid getting a merchant account.

Downsides of Special Events

- Special events typically occur on Friday nights or over the weekend so you have to be willing to give up some of your weekends to succeed with this sales channel. This may work to your benefit if that's the only time you have to dedicate to your food business, but in some cases the time away from friends and family may mean this is not the best sales channel for you.

- Special events are special for a reason and that means they come with more stress. This might not be the right sales channel for you if you really don't want to work with high-maintenance brides or obsessive party planners.

Things to Know About Special Events

- Customers want to make sure they're getting the best possible food for their special day and will likely request a tasting with you before signing a contract.
- When it comes to contracts for orders that will require significant cost on your part to complete, it is advisable to require a deposit. The contract should also stipulate when final payment is due. Experienced food entrepreneurs recommend that final payment be due at least two weeks before the special event. In the final days before the event your customers may be so busy with all the final details that they'll simply overlook getting a check ready to give to you and trying to track them down afterwards for payment can be difficult to manage.
- Know if you're required to charge sales tax for your products.
- If you will be delivering your products consider adding in a delivery fee to cover the cost of your gas and your time.
- Networking and word-of-mouth marketing is the cheapest form of special events advertising. Let everyone know that you are starting up a food company that will feature items that are great for special events. Consider offering a "friends and family" discount to encourage people to start ordering and to share your name with their friends and family.
- It helps to have a strong web presence that includes pictures of items you have made for special events and testimonials from happy customers. Even if you're just starting out, make some samples and have professional-quality pictures taken for your site. Your website will likely be the first impression your

customers get of your business and you want it to wow them so that they call you to schedule a tasting.

Special Events Startup Costs

In addition to your business registration, kitchen rental, marketing collateral, and other initial startup costs, for special events you will need to be willing to cover the costs of tastings for potential clients. You may also need to invest in additional equipment, such as a cake stands or serving dishes, based on your specific business.

Need A Little Extra Help?

If you need an extra set of hands from time to time to help you with your production or product sales it is possible to easily – and legally – hire temporary help. As long as the person you hire doesn't earn more than $599 from your company in a calendar year you can simply hire them and pay them with a company check but you don't have to report the hire to the IRS or pay employer-related taxes. Be sure to keep careful notes, including a copy of all checks paid to that temporary employee. This paper trail will be helpful in proving you obeyed the law should the IRS ever audit you.

If you're looking for more than temporary help and plan on paying someone more than $599 in a calendar year then you will need to hire the person as an employee. Even if you're just hiring a part-time employee you still need to verify that they are legally allowed to work and you will be responsible for filing all employee withholding taxes. The IRS website (www.irs.gov) outlines these steps in more detail. Some accounting software programs like Quicken and QuickBooks may be able to help you manage your payroll accordingly or you may choose to outsource your payroll needs to a company that specializes in payroll services and will ensure that your quarterly state and federal employment paperwork is filed properly and on time.

How They Got Their Start
Half Pint Ice Cream

Sometimes your first job turns out to be your calling. That's been the case for Cle Franklin at least. Her first job as a teenager was working at an ice cream store and it was the job she went back to throughout high-school and college vacations. "I simply love ice cream," she says, "and the customer service aspect of the job was always fun."

Fast forward several years and Cle, now in her early 20's, moved across the country to a new city and immediately started scouting out her local coffee stores, grocery stores, and ice cream stores. She easily found new favorites for the first two but couldn't find any local stores that made their own ice cream. Her only choice was 'big box' ice cream stores whose ice cream, in Cle's opinion based on what she was used to, left much to be desired. Not being able to find any artisan ice cream stores in her new city planted the seed in Cle's mind that there might very well be a market for it. However, as she was not too long out of college and with limited savings, it wasn't an idea she could act on so she put it aside and took a job in the hospitality industry.

Five years later the idea was still there, niggling at the back of her mind. At the same time, Cle had grown bored with her hospitality position and was ready to leave. Since she knew she didn't want to open up an ice cream store due to the startup costs involved, it dawned on Cle that she'd never seen ice cream sold at any of the local farmers' markets. Was this due to the fact that there wasn't a market for artisan ice cream in this city, Cle wondered? But at the same time, the startup costs to try and sell ice cream at a farmers' market were so much lower then opening up a store, she figured it couldn't hurt to try.

Just because she had the idea didn't mean she really knew how to start implementing it. She took a position at a local bakery to help cover her personal costs and spent three frantic months working close to full-time while also trying to learn everything there was to know about starting up a farmer's market ice cream business. "I put in a ton of phone calls," Cle remembers. "First I called up the Farmers' Market Alliance and they told me what I needed to even be considered for the market from a health code standpoint, which directed me to the health department who I called up and they told me I needed an approved kitchen space before I could start anything else. I literally had no clue where to start the process but the people I talked with were very helpful."

Since her product was something the farmers' markets weren't used to carrying, she was initially accepted into two markets which meant she quickly had to find equipment on her very limited budget. "I think I could have planned better financially," Cle says, "but my startup costs weren't that much. I bought a lot of stuff for my farmers' market booth at Goodwill. Since I was going for a handmade look I didn't need slick-looking stuff." One of Cle's biggest expenses, aside from her health permitting and commercial kitchen rent, was an ice cream cart she bought. The cart enables Cle to store her ice cream at the correct temperature during the market, is easily mobile, and still fits the handmade look she's created for her company, Half Pint Ice Cream (a fairly tongue-in-cheek name given Cle's 'less than tall' height).

Cle admits that her startup costs were less then $4,000 but that every little purchase was agonizing. "I wasn't sure what was going to happen with the business so I didn't want to invest in expensive equipment. Part of me wishes I had invested in a big fancy ice cream machine from the beginning because it just makes a better product and can do double or even triple the production volume. But at the same time I think being forced to work with my little ice cream makers that first year helped me learn how to make a better product."

Cle spent much of that first summer shuttling her old Volvo station wagon, stuffed to the brim with farmer' market booth materials, her cart, and all her ice cream, to two farmers' markets, to her shared kitchen space, and then onto her job. Even though ice cream at a farmers' market was new to most people, from the very first market customers fell in love with Cle's rich handmade ice cream and

delicious flavor combinations. *She soon added a third farmers'*
market to her schedule which required her to quit her bakery job
and by the end of that first summer she had just about broken even.

While Cle's business became more or less full-time in the summer,
there's a large seasonal aspect to it given that people don't want ice
cream as much in the winter. When her markets ended in the fall,
Cle found herself out of a job and out of an income source. "I knew
that I wanted to go home and visit family for the holidays since I
hadn't been able to go home at all over the summer," Cle says, "so I
called up my old employer and asked them if they needed temporary
help." Cle ended up working about 20 hours a week during the
winter which was just enough to pay her rent and other financial
obligations but wasn't enough to keep her from going a little crazy.
"I'm the type of person who likes to keep busy," Cle says, "and I think
that's true of most people who start their own businesses. Not
working all the time in the winter was really tough on me and I
honestly think between the downtime and the weather I became
depressed. I've never been so happy to see summer come back
around as I was that year!"

Before her second summer season began, Cle bit the bullet and
bought that big expensive $30,000 industrial ice cream machine
she'd wished for her first year. But since she was, as always, keeping
an eye on expenses, she didn't pay nearly that much for it. "I found
the machine on EBay®," Cle says. "A guy had bought it from a
franchised ice cream store that was going out of business so I was
able to get a great deal on it. Granted, shipping it cost me close to
$1000. Plus, when I first plugged it in the compressor died so that
took another couple of thousand dollars to fix. But at the end of the
day I probably spent $8,000-$9,000 on a machine that has literally
changed my business more than anything else. Plus, I can't even put
a price tag on what it's done for my sanity!"

The new machine allows her to produce twice the ice cream in
about half the time. At the end of each week's markets during her
first season Cle would not have a scoop of ice cream left. The new
machine gives her the ability to make more then enough for five

markets. In fact, she even has enough production capacity that she's been able to add in catering for special events. Even though she hasn't done any special events marketing, she consistently books clients simply through word-of-mouth referrals. "For me special events are great because I know I'm going to get paid regardless of what the weather is like," Cle says. "At farmers markets how much I make is very dependent on the weather but at special events they're contracted to pay me a certain amount even if no one wants ice cream. It's nice to be able to somewhat predict how much money I'm going to make."

Over the past few years Half Pint Ice Cream has more than tripled its revenue, it now has a loyal farmers market following, and it has grown to the point where Cle now has to turn away business. Her company is right on the cusp of being nearly impossible for Cle to do all the production, the markets, and the special events on her own. "I did hire someone for a few months during the busy season and that was a wakeup call to me that the right person can do this job. I'm not the only one who can make and sell my ice cream. At first I was nervous all the time when (the employee) first started but I finally realized that she's totally capable. Plus, it finally dawned on me that what's the worst that can really happen? All the ice cream can melt...ok, it wouldn't be great but it's certainly not life or death!"

Having someone help out has given Cle a more balanced life and lets her enjoy a little bit of summer but the seasonal aspect of her business still means that she's working like crazy during the summer and has time on her hands in the winter. On the plus side, Cle says that the seasonality of her business means that she's always excited and rejuvenated to start a new season and she has been able to work on inventing new flavors in the winter in addition to actually working on other hobbies. But the flip side is that money is always a concern since in a seasonal business you have to work hard in season to help fund the off months.

"Overall I really like that it's a seasonal business," Cle says. "If I lived in a warmer region where I could keep the business going year-round I think it would be nice, but for now and given that I don't want to move, I'm pretty happy with what I've created. I do wish I could find something that would keep me excited and engaged in the winter and I know it's out there – I just have to figure out what it is!" In the meantime, Cle has dreams of growing Half Pint Ice Cream down the road. "My ice cream cart can be hooked up to a bike so I've thought about having someone bike up and down the beach during the summer months selling my ice cream. Or maybe I'll have branded ice cream carts in strategic parts of the city!" The options, it seems, are limitless!

BRANDING:
DESIGNING YOUR LOOK

It's important to remember that people shop for food first with their eyes. Your product has to look good for them to want to try it. Part of what they look at is not just the food item itself but the entire presentation and packaging of your product and company. Think of it like this, if a company has what looks like a great empanada for sale but their packaging is terrible you'll likely steer clear of it. An obvious example, yes, but everything in and around your product helps tell a story to your customers and you want to make sure it's the right story.

Creating Your Logo

Just like your company name, your company logo will be on everything the customer sees. Whether it's on your banner at a farmers market, on a sticker placed on your packaging, or on the business card that you hand out to people, your logo helps build an impression about who your company is and what it stands for. Spend some time thinking about what you want your company to represent so that the logo will suit it. Is your company fun and whimsical? Is it sophisticated and luxurious? Understand your company and your customers so that you can understand the type of logo you're looking for.

As far as designing the logo, you can certainly hire a graphic artist to make the logo for you, but if you're trying to save money take a look at your family and friends first. Perhaps someone you know works in graphic design and wouldn't mind taking on a little side project or maybe you have a neighbor who has an artistic flare. One thrifty entrepreneur had her 8-year-old son design her logo. Since her company was targeted to children and had a playful brand, her son's logo captured that probably better then most professional graphic artists could have. Better yet, it only cost her a peanut-butter sandwich!

Websites: Online All The Time

Your website is your company's voice and image around the clock. Even when you're sleeping your website will tell people about your company and provide them with contact information. Regardless of whether you offer online retail sales, a website should be one of the pieces of the puzzle you plan to incorporate into the new business.

There are three main ways you can get a website set up. The easiest, but most expensive, is to contract with a web developer who will be able to get your site registered and up and running with minimal hands-on work from you. The main thing you'll have to do is write the checks to fund this. Depending on how complex a site you want, a web developer may charge anywhere from $1500 to upwards of $10,000 or more for your site. Of course if you have a friend or family member, or know of a student with strong web skills, you may be able to get a break on the rate.

If you do hire a web developer make sure your money is being spent well and that your website is being optimized for web searches. This means that if someone types a word in their search engine that is related to your business then your company website will come up early in their search results. Known as Search Engine Optimization or SEO, this will help make sure that your website will be easy to find and get in front of customers' eyes.

Another easy and increasingly popular option for small businesses is to set up a website via a blog site like WordPress® (www.wordpress.com) or Blogger® (www.blogger.com). The upside to this is that these programs require very little technical knowledge and you can quickly and easily update your own site. Plus these sites currently allow you to host your site with them for free. If you go through a blog site you will have two naming options. You can either purchase a domain name (your website name) directly through the blog or you can use the website address they provide free of charge. If you go the latter route, you will have a web address along the lines of www.yourcompanyname.blogname.com. This can be a mouthful for people to remember, make it harder to find your site online, and in some people's mind makes your business look less professional. For this reason, if you decide to use a blog site to create and update your website, it's recommended that you purchase a domain name of your own. Keep in mind that a blog site may not have all the functionality you desire in a website such as an ability to incorporate an online shopping cart or Flash graphics.

If you don't want to use a blog program or web developer, it is possible to design a website on your own. In order to do this you will need to purchase a domain name and get your site hosted. The specifics about setting up your own website go beyond the scope of this book. Certain companies like GoDaddy® (www.godaddy.com) and Intuit® (www.intuit.com) now allow you to purchase a domain name, get your site hosted, and set up a basic website. While these do not allow for the most dynamic of sites, it is a good starter guide and relatively inexpensive when compared to hiring your own web developer.

Packaging

If you plan to sell any of your products pre-packaged or if you'll need to make deliveries which will require packaging, the packaging you choose will speak volumes about your product even after it's out of your hands. Think about some of your favorite retailers, do they use a certain color ribbon to tie all their boxes with? Do they always use a certain sticker? What do you think about when you see that ribbon or sticker? The packaging surrounding your products will help support the brand you've created. If your company focuses on all-natural products perhaps an eco-friendly box tied with natural raffia ribbon is the way to go. In the example of the 'playful' child-centric company mentioned earlier, the company's packaging included a temporary tattoo of her logo that children just loved and it strengthened the connection in customers' minds that hers was a company focused on children.

Packaging can get expensive but it doesn't necessarily have to be. When you're starting out, you might be able to find the necessary packaging at local kitchen supply stores or craft shops. Appendix IX on page 130 includes information about other packaging sources that may be helpful for packaging ideas or as good places to purchase packaging.

When you're looking for packaging for food items make sure that the packaging has been approved by the FDA for safe food contact.

> ### *Packaging Tip*
> *When you're first starting out and looking to save money, consider using basic white office labels (available at office supply stores) for your labels. You can put a graphic of your logo onto the label fairly simply and easily change text such as ingredients and nutritional analysis as needed for your products. This way you can print out labels as you need them and you don't have to purchase professionally printed labels, which are typically sold in minimum quantities of several hundred, until your business needs that many labels on a regular basis.*

You

You and anyone who works for you is also part of your brand. Anytime you talk with customers whether over the phone or in person, you are adding to that story they're building about your company. If a potential customer comes by for a tasting and you're flustered and covered in beet juice it doesn't say a lot about your organization or your ability to handle the pressure of a special event. If however when you meet the customer you're calm, present yourself well, and look put-together it's going to leave a much better impression. Anytime you're in front of customers, whether at tastings, farmers markets, craft shows, or any other event, you're helping to tell the story about your company. Make no mistake, you are part of the brand you've created!

How They Got Their Start
Intrigue Chocolates Co.

In hindsight it may seem obvious that a junior high student who spent his free time making candies in his home kitchen would grow up to become a chocolatier. Aaron Barthel, however, took the long way of getting there. He studied science ecology - with an emphasis on botany- at St. John's University in Minnesota, spent a few months selling cutlery after graduation, and then took a job at Great Harvest Bakery when he realized that he didn't want to work in either the field or a lab. Although he didn't have any professional baking experience, within a week of being hired he was promoted to 'dough master' – a title Aaron gave himself to describe his new role of making all the dough for the bakery. "Bread is fascinating to work with because it's a living organism. I spent time experimenting with flavors and adding new products to their menu," Aaron remembers. He also spent nine months volunteering at a local micro-brewery. "I guess I was working with micro-ecologies after all!"

Despite enjoying frequent deliveries of fresh bread, Aaron's mother was afraid he'd give up on his botany background altogether so she bought him a subscription to a horticulture magazine. In one of the first issues Aaron received there was a recipe for Orange Mint truffles. The recipe caught Aaron's attention but without any orange mint on hand, he experimented with some habanera chilies he'd grown and dried the year before. With very minor tweaking over the this initial creation became his signature Jamaican HOT Chocolate Truffle, inspired by traditional Mexican spiced chocolates. From that first experiment Aaron was instantly hooked on chocolate in this form. "I loved playing with flavors in combination with chocolate and using my knowledge of plants to create those flavors naturally." Despite his love of working with chocolate, he never thought about turning it into a business.

Plans for graduate school lead to a cross-country move, but Aaron found himself working at the YMCA and no longer quite as interested in going back to college for a while. He was sharing the occasional batch of truffles with members of the YMCA, when friends who were starting up a boxed lunch catering business asked if he'd be willing to join them part-time to make his truffles and breads for their company. "It was perfect timing for me; I had needed a new plan and this would allow me to explore new flavors! My friends at Madres Kitchen allowed me to use my own business name, Intrigue Chocolates Co., under the umbrella of their own," Aaron says. "I knew I needed to start my branding from the very beginning because that's really all you have as a small company. It's how people will recognize your products and it gives you a way to grow." With the help of a friend at the YMCA who was a graphic artist and photographer (and an aerobics instructor!), Aaron was able to get a professionally designed logo at minimal cost. "All of these friends with talent came together at the right time to learn new skills, share information, exchange some business, and help each other's companies grow."

Aaron spent a dizzying 18 months creating his truffles and bread part-time for the catering company while simultaneously working at the YMCA and also as the program coordinator for the ROOTS Young Adult Shelter. (Aaron readily admits his schedule was absolutely insane.) After that, business for the catering company started to slow down which in turn meant fewer hours for Aaron. Making lemonade out of lemons, or in this case, sweets out of a sour situation, Aaron decided to split Intrigue Chocolates Co. off entirely and moved his operations into a shared kitchen space.

In addition to his love of chocolate, Aaron has always enjoyed fine wine and even conceived of his chocolates as a natural pairing partner for wine. When the catering company business was slowing down, Aaron used some of his free time to take a quick trip to a neighboring wine region. While there, Aaron left some truffle samples and brochures with the wineries but didn't think much of it so was very much surprised when several weeks later a marketing specialist from one of the wineries contacted him asking for more samples. The winery eventually brought Intrigue Chocolates into their big Valentine's Day Event – Red Wine & Chocolate – and the response to Aaron's chocolates was so overwhelming that the winery asked Intrigue Chocolates Co. to come to their winery for weekly wine/chocolate pairing events where Aaron could also sell gift boxes of truffles. "At the time, those event sales were the mainstay of the business," Aaron says. The relationship proved beneficial to both the winery and Aaron for several years until a change in the winery's business strategy meant Aaron had to start looking elsewhere to sell his goodies. He didn't need to worry about it for long; by the end of the following week he had signed up two new wineries, one of which was directly across the street from the old winery.

Looking back, Aaron says that one of the biggest hurdles he faced was in determining the right price for his product. He said he balked when he first realized how much he had to charge for his chocolates in order to break even. "I came to realize that small companies should never compete with the large organizations on price," he says. "If you try to compete on price you will lose because they can always make a product cheaper then you. They can afford to take a loss here to make a gain there or to push out the competition. Instead, you need to compete on quality and tell your customers the story about what makes your product special. People who appreciate handcrafted artisan quality are your target customers. People who care more about price then quality are going to shop elsewhere but that's fine. You simply focus on the people who care about what you bring to the table."

In addition to his winery partnerships, Aaron grew the business by partnering with local stores and clubs around the city that held chocolate and wine tastings. "As a small chocolatier I really felt that we had to differentiate ourselves and the way we did that was by creating over 90 flavors of chocolate truffles, and each one can dance with a different wine!" The tastings generated so much business for him that after about three years Aaron left his job at the homeless shelter (he had left the YMCA position almost two and a half years earlier, and the caterers a year after that) in order to devote all his time to Intrigue Chocolates Co. Even though he's kept marketing to a minimum – using things like FaceBook®, a company *blog, and e-newsletters – Intrigue Chocolates Co. continues to grow. In addition to the tasting events, the company works with a select number of caterers, restaurants, and event planners. The company's website is also adding new customers almost daily. In fact, Intrigue Chocolates Co. has literally outgrown its kitchen space and Aaron recently signed a lease for his own work space. While the space he rented is in the heart of the city and is perfect for what Aaron anticipates, it does require that he actually build the commercial kitchen. That means not only getting contractors' bids and city permitting, but also getting the final approval from city health inspectors, which is not an easy task. In the meantime, Aaron continues to create his chocolates in the shared kitchen space he's rented for years while also overseeing construction on the new space and knocking on bank doors to try and secure additional financing. "I won't lie," he says with a nervous laugh, "I'm terrified. Really excited but also terrified!"*

To many, the idea of writing a business plan – especially for a part-time business – sounds either overwhelming or just plain tedious. But even for a part-time food business, a business plan can get you started off on the right foot. The business plan will help you clarify and organize all the ideas you have running through your head about the business and it forces you to take a hard look at the finances of the business to make sure that you're pricing your products in such a way that you can actually make money. The plan for a part-time food business doesn't need to be overly complex, however it should, at a minimum, include the following sections. For a sample business plan see Appendix I on page 109.

Company Description

This section should outline what you envision your company becoming, a high-level view of what you plan on offering, and any guiding principles you want to incorporate into the business such as a commitment to use only all-natural or locally-sourced ingredients. Briefly include information about your existing or anticipated business format and health code certifications. This section should also include information on any risks your business will face so you can be aware of potential issues before they happen. It's also a good idea to use this section to outline goals you have for this year and future years. Don't be afraid to reach for the sky and include some stretch goals!

Target Market

You need to understand who your customers will likely be in order to offer them products they'll value and want to buy. Are your customers price conscious or are they planning a special event and so have larger budgets? Do your customers care more about quality ingredients or how a product is packaged? What 'need' does your product help fill for customers (yes, looking for a tasty delicacy or the perfect St. Louis style BBQ sauce does qualify as a 'need'). Understanding your customers , and what motivates them, enables you to see the world through their eyes and create a sales and marketing strategy that will speak to them.

Competition

What other products or companies do your customers have to choose from? Including information about direct competitors will help you better understand how you can differentiate your company and how you might be better able to add more value in your customers' eyes.

Product Portfolio

With a firm understanding of who your customers are and what competition you face, this is where you will briefly describe the products you are planning to offer and key selling points that differentiate your products from competitors.

Sales Channels

Use this area to outline the sales channels you plan on using to sell your products. If possible, include information about all sales channels you hope to use during the first year even if some may not be avenues you pursue right away.

Packaging

Packaging is an extension of your brand so if you plan to package any of your products think about how this presentation will be viewed by your customers. This section should describe how you envision your products being packaged with an eye to your target market, ie customers who want organic products or price-sensitive consumers.

If you are packaging any of your products be sure to check with your local health department to see if they require an ingredients label or nutritional analysis on pre-packaged items. If you do need a nutritional analysis, a quick internet search will result in a number of companies, such as Compu-Food Analysis, Inc (www.compufoodanalysis.com), that can perform this service for you and provide you with accurate data in

[78]

the format required by health authorities. Even if you don't have to include this information, it's not a bad idea to include an ingredients label so as to avoid potential food allergy complications.

Marketing

Marketing is how you get the word out that your company is open and ready for business. Every company markets itself whether it's through advertisements or simple networking among friends. It's now easier than ever to tell people about your company thanks to social media marketing through a company blog and networking sites like FaceBook® and Twitter®. Don't underestimate the power of Google Adwords® and targeted advertisements on FaceBook or other sites even if traditional print or radio advertising is too expensive or not a good fit for your company.

A Note About PR

Free press is a great thing if it's positive and in a publication your target market sees. If you're interested in trying to get press for your company, PR agencies will promise you the moon but it may cost you the sun and they don't always deliver. For a small part-time business, it's possible to save your money and try to attract free press on your own with a little work.

Start by drawing up a list of print and online publications that fit with the target market you're hoping to attract and try to find out who covers the items related to your product. Depending on what type of business you're starting, this may be the food editor or possibly even a markets editor. When in doubt, call up the publication and ask them to point you in the right direction.

Don't discount blogs as they're a very powerful resource for getting the word out about your company. Research blogs that your target market might be reading and add them to your list of

A Note About PR, Cont'd

publications to contact. Once this list is complete, the next step is to get your product in front of these key people. The good news is that free food is almost always appreciated so cook up your best batch and drop it off at the publications' offices (or mail the product if need be). Since you likely won't make it past the receptionist or front door security without an appointment, be sure to include information about your company with the samples you leave. You may want to consider leaving samples for the receptionist/front door security as well to sweeten the deal! Highlight anything different or unusual about your product or company that will give the publication a reason to tell their readers about you. Also be sure to let the receptionist/front door security know that the box contains food samples so it doesn't sit for three days before making it to the right desk. There is certainly no guarantee this will get you any press but the only cost to you is your time and the ingredients you use so you may decide it's worth a try.

While most publications try to keep their advertising and editorial departments separate, it is not uncommon for companies that advertise with a specific publication to receive more press. If you plan to do any advertising with a print or online publication, ask your advertising representative to direct you to the editorial staff member who handles products like yours. An introduction from the advertising representative will usually carry more weight as publications want to keep their advertisers happy so they'll keep advertising. As with all things PR, there's certainly no guarantee you'll get press but it never hurts to leverage any inside tracks you may develop.

Obviously, this is an overview of PR and for more in-depth information you should either work with a PR expert or look at one of the hundreds of books written on the subject available through your bookstore or library.

Cost Analysis

Product pricing is a key component to building a successful business but it's one that too many people simply skim over. It's not unusual for food entrepreneurs not to know their true product costs and simply charge what they anticipate to be a fair price for an item. However, if you don't know how much it costs to make the product then you can't know if the price you charge will actually make you any money.

To determine your product costs follow the steps below for each of your products. A sample product spreadsheet is on page 83 for reference and a product cost worksheet to use with your products is available in Appendix IV starting on page 123. The following information is based on the fictional company Greta's Gluten-Free Goodies outlined in the Sample Business Plan in Appendix I beginning on page 109.

Step 1A: Ingredient Unit Cost: Divide the total cost you paid for each ingredient (including tax if applicable) by the total number of units bought. For example, if a 5LB bag of gluten-free flour costs $4.80 then the unit cost is $.06 per ounce:

> 5lbx16 =80 ounces
> (there are 16 ounces in a pound so this converts the units to ounces)
> $4.80 (total unit cost)/80 ounces = $.06 per ounce

Step 1B: Product Ingredient Cost: To determine the unit cost of each ingredient in each product, multiply the number of units you use in a recipe with the corresponding Ingredient Unit Cost from Step 1A. Using the above example, if you use 5 ounces of gluten-free flour in your recipe then the Product Ingredient Cost is $.30
> 5(ounces of flour) x $.06(Ingredient Unit Cost) = $.30

Step 1C: Total Ingredient Cost: Add together all the Product Ingredient Costs to arrive at the Total Ingredient Cost.

Step 1D: Per Piece Total Ingredient Cost: Divide the Total Ingredient Cost by the number of units each recipe makes to get your Per Piece

Total Ingredient Cost. If your Total Ingredient Cost comes to $2.19 and the recipe makes 12 pieces then your Per Piece Total Ingredient Cost is $.18 per piece.

$$\$2.19(\text{Total Ingredient Cost})/12(\text{Total Units}) = \$.18$$

Note: If you are selling your products individually or without packaging you can skip Steps 2 and 3.

Step 2: Packaging Cost: Add together any packaging costs for the product including bags, stickers, ribbons (per inch or foot), etc on a per unit basis to arrive at your total packaging cost per product. If you will be packaging your items in a bag that costs $.06 and will include a label that costs $.29 then your total packaging cost is $.35 per unit.

$$\$.06(\text{bag}) + \$.29(\text{sticker}) = \$.35$$

Step 3: Total Product Cost: To arrive at your Total Product Cost, multiply the number of products per package by the Total Ingredient Cost and add in the Total Packaging Cost. Using the former example once again, if you plan to sell three items together, each of which costs you $.18 to produce, in packaging that costs $.35 then your Total Product Cost will be $.89.

$$3(\text{units}) \times \$.18 \ (\text{Total Ingredient Cost}) = \$.54$$
$$\$.54 + \$.35(\text{Total Packaging Cost}) = \$.89$$

Greta's Gluten-Free Goodies
Product Cost and Pricing

Chocolate Inferno Cookies
Product Cost

Ingredients	Amount Used (ounces)	Per Unit Cost	Total
gluten-free flour	5	$ 0.30	$ 1.50
cocoa powder	0.33	$ 0.13	$ 0.04
butter	8	$ 0.04	$ 0.32
eggs (per egg)	2	$ 0.15	$ 0.30
cayenne pepper	0.12	$ 0.29	$ 0.03
Total Ingredient Cost			$ 2.19
Per Piece Product Ingredient Cost (12 pieces)			$ 0.18

Farmers' Market Packaging

Packaging	Amount Used	Per Unit Cost	Total
Labels	1	$ 0.29	$ 0.29
Bags	1	$ 0.06	$ 0.06
Total Product Packaging Cost			$ 0.35

Number of Cookies per package	3
Total Per Package Ingredient Cost	$ 0.54
Total Product Cost with Packaging	$ 0.89

Special Events

Packaging	Amount Used	Per Unit Cost	Total
Labels	1	$ 0.29	$ 0.29
Box	1	$ 0.36	$ 0.36
Ribbon	.25 yards	$1.89/yd	$ 0.47
Total Product Packaging Cost			$ 1.12

Number of Cookies per package	12
Total Per Package Ingredient Cost	$ 2.19
Total Product Cost with Packaging	$ 3.31

Pricing Your Products

You now know exactly how much it costs you to produce your products and what price, at a minimum, you need to sell them for in order to break even. However, this amount does not take into account the other big variable cost – the time it takes for you to make the product. Some people take this Total Product Cost a step further by adding in the cost of the time spent making and packaging the product. With cooking and baking though, this can be a harder figure to determine as you will need to time yourself to know exactly how many minutes it takes to make one unit of product and how much time it takes to package that item.

An easier formula that is the industry rule of thumb is to multiply your Total Product Cost by four for retail pricing and by two for wholesale pricing. This would mean that the Chocolate Inferno Cookies on page 83, packaged three to a bag as in the Farmers' Market packaging example, would sell at the retail price of $3.56 or $1.78 when sold wholesale. This formula should help account for the time you put into making and packaging the product as well as help cover the cost of overhead such as your kitchen rent, electricity, etc.

Of course, after you arrive at your prices you need to make sure that the price isn't either too low or too high for the marketplace and whether this product takes substantial time to create. The above formula provides you with a starting point for price and you can raise or lower it based on information specific to your products and your market.

Adding In Your Time

If you want to add in the cost of your time to your Total Product Cost you first need to decide what hourly wage you'd like to be 'paid' and then how long it takes you to make one individual unit of product and package it. Since it's not often possible to make just one cookie, for example, time yourself while making a regular batch and divide that time by the number of units the batch produces. Then time yourself on how long it takes you to package up one item. Combine your times for the one package and divide that by 60 in order to get the percentage of an hour that the process takes you. For example, if it takes you 16 minutes to bake and package your cookies then it would have taken you 27% of an hour. Multiply that percentage by your hourly wage and add that to your Total Product Cost.

The tricky part is whether or not you should include in time when you aren't actively working on the product but it can't yet be packaged or sold. For example, do you include the time it took for the cookies to cool even if you were able to work on something else during that time? This is obviously a judgment call you have to make for your own business.

Cash Forecasting

Knowing how much to charge for your products is one thing but before starting up your business you should have a good idea of how much you'll be spending on a monthly basis and how much you anticipate making. Business plan books will tell you that when starting a business you need to build out an Income Statement and Balance Sheet. While helpful, for a small part-time business the focus should really be on Cash Forecasting. How much money or liquidity the business has at any given time, is incredibly important to a small business as a healthy cash position will enable you to pay your bills on time and keep the day-to-day business running. Even if you anticipate great sales in the future, without cash in the bank you won't be able to pay the rent tomorrow.

Developing a Cash Forecast will show you how and when money will be spent alongside how and when you anticipate receiving cash from sales. Then you can make sure that the two add up so that your business always has cash available when needed.

When creating a Cash Forecast, the first thing you need to know is what your monthly Operating Costs will most likely be. Operating Costs differ from your Startup Costs in that they typically occur on a monthly or otherwise regular basis whereas Startup Costs are one-time initial upfront costs to get the business up and running such as your business licenses and web development costs. There are two types of Operating Costs - Fixed Operating Costs and Variable Operating Costs. Fixed Operating Costs are things that will occur every month regardless of whether or not you have any sales. These are things like your phone bill, your monthly web hosting fees, and any rent for your kitchen space. Variable Operating Costs are dependent on how much product you are making, such as the cost of your ingredients, or discretionary expenses that you can easily increase or decrease such as how much you spend on Advertising. It's important to remember the difference between the two because if your sales go up your Fixed Operating Costs are going to remain unchanged but your Variable Operating Costs that correspond with your product, mainly ingredient and packaging costs, will increase. On the same note, if you aren't making a lot of product then your Variable Operating Costs will be minimal but your Fixed Operating Costs will stay the same.

The following page provides an example of the Fixed and Variable Costs for the fictional company Greta's Gluten-free Goodies which operates as a part-time seasonal farmers' market business. From this you can see how Greta anticipates what her average monthly cash needs will be over and above her Startup Costs.

Greta's Gluten-Free Goodies

	May	June	July	Aug	Sept	Oct
Fixed Costs						
Kitchen Facilities	$ 550	$ 550	$ 550	$ 550	$ 550	$ 550
Office Supplies	$ -	$ 50	$ -	$ -	$ 50	$ -
Telephone/Internet	$ 110	$ 110	$ 110	$ 110	$ 110	$ 110
Accounting	$ 40	$ 40	$ 40	$ 40	$ 40	$ 40
Website	$ 35	$ 35	$ 35	$ 35	$ 35	$ 35
Total Monthly Fixed Costs	**$ 735**	**$ 785**	**$ 735**	**$ 735**	**$ 785**	**$ 735**
Variable Costs						
Ingredients	$ 250	$ 300	$ 350	$ 350	$ 300	$ 250
Marketing						
Farmers Market Minimum Fee	$ 120	$ 140	$ 160	$ 160	$ 140	$ 120
Print Advertising	$ -	$ -	$ -	$ -	$ -	$ -
Online Advertising	$ 25	$ 25	$ 25	$ 25	$ 25	$ 25
Newsletter/e-newsletter	$ -	$ -	$ -	$30	$ -	$ -
Marketing Postcards	$ 150	$ -	$ -	$ -	$ -	$ -
Photography	$ 250	$ -	$ -	$ -	$ -	$ -
Samples	$ 6	$ 7	$ 8	$ 8	$ 7	$ 6
Total Variable Costs	**$ 801**	**$ 472**	**$ 543**	**$ 573**	**$ 472**	**$ 401**
Other Costs						
Packaging Costs						
Labels	$ 350	$ -	$ -	$ -	$ -	$ -
Bags	$ 200	$ -	$ -	$ -	$ -	$ -
Ribbon	$ 150	$ -	$ -	$ -	$ -	$ -
Total Other Costs	**$ 700**	**$ -**	**$ -**	**$ -**	**$ -**	**$ -**
Total Operating Costs	**$ 2,236**	**$ 1,257**	**$ 1,278**	**$ 1,308**	**$ 1,257**	**$ 1,136**

As you can see in the above example, Greta's Gluten-Free Goodies anticipates that the Fixed Operating Costs will remain the same every month during the summer farmers' market season but the Variable Costs, mainly the ingredients and minimum fees owed to the farmers' market association, will rise during the peak of summer and decrease during the Spring and Fall when the weather is less reliable and attendance at the farmers markets is typically lower.

It's also important to note that Greta's Gluten-Free Goodies has taken into account the fact that there are several costs that will have to be paid in May for things like packaging, photography, and marketing postcards. Even though these items may be used all season, it will be necessary for Greta's Gluten-Free Goodies to have either the cash on hand or a business credit card to pay for those items before the farmers' markets really get going.

Once you understand your monthly expenses, you now need to add in what you think you will sell on a monthly basis to get a true Cash

Forecast. Without any historic data behind you, this really is your best guess as to how much you may sell during any given month taking into account how much of the product you can physically make. For example it's no use putting into your projection that you'll sell 8000 units a month if it is physically impossible for you to produce that much. One recommendation is to make three projections based on 1) a worst-case sales scenario, 2) a 'real' scenario based on what you actually anticipate selling, and 3) a best-case sales scenario. Keep in mind that as your sales change in each of those scenarios so too will some of your variable costs. Note the change in the cost of ingredients and farmers market fee in each of the following three sample projections.

Greta's Gluten-Free Goodies
Realistic Cash Forecast

	May	June	July	Aug	Sept	Oct
Fixed Costs						
Kitchen Facilities	$ 550	$ 550	$ 550	$ 550	$ 550	$ 550
Office Supplies	$ -	$ 50	$ -	$ -	$ 50	$ -
Telephone/Internet	$ 110	$ 110	$ 110	$ 110	$ 110	$ 110
Accounting	$ 40	$ 40	$ 40	$ 40	$ 40	$ 40
Website	$ 35	$ 35	$ 35	$ 35	$ 35	$ 35
Total Monthly Fixed Costs	**$ 735**	**$ 785**	**$ 735**	**$ 735**	**$ 785**	**$ 735**
Variable Costs						
Ingredients	$ 250	$ 300	$ 350	$ 350	$ 300	$ 250
Marketing						
Farmers' Market Minimum Fee	$ 120	$ 140	$ 160	$ 160	$ 140	$ 120
Print Advertising	$ -	$ -	$ -	$ -	$ -	$ -
Online Advertising	$ 25	$ 25	$ 25	$ 25	$ 25	$ 25
Newsletter/e-newsletter	$ -	$ -	$ -	$30	$ -	$ -
Marketing Postcards	$ 150	$ -	$ -	$ -	$ -	$ -
Photography	$ 250	$ -	$ -	$ -	$ -	$ -
Samples	$ 6	$ 7	$ 8	$ 8	$ 7	$ 6
Total Variable Costs	**$ 801**	**$ 472**	**$ 543**	**$ 573**	**$ 472**	**$ 401**
Other Costs						
Packaging Costs						
Labels	$ 350	$ -	$ -	$ -	$ -	$ -
Bags	$ 200	$ -	$ -	$ -	$ -	$ -
Ribbon	$ 150	$ -	$ -	$ -	$ -	$ -
Total Other Costs	**$ 700**	**$ -**	**$ -**	**$ -**	**$ -**	**$ -**
Total Operating Costs	**$ 2,236**	**$ 1,257**	**$ 1,278**	**$ 1,308**	**$ 1,257**	**$ 1,136**
Projected Sales	**$ 1,200**	**$ 1,600**	**$ 2,000**	**$ 2,000**	**$ 1,800**	**$ 1,300**
Net Income (Sales - Costs)	**$ (1,036)**	**$ 343**	**$ 722**	**$ 692**	**$ 543**	**$ 164**
Starting Cash On Hand	**$ 5,000**	**$ 3,964**	**$ 4,307**	**$ 5,029**	**$ 5,721**	**$ 6,264**
+ Net Income	**$ 3,964**	**$ 4,307**	**$ 5,029**	**$ 5,721**	**$ 6,264**	**$ 6,428**
Ending Cash On Hand	**$ 3,964**	**$ 4,307**	**$ 5,029**	**$ 5,721**	**$ 6,264**	**$ 6,428**

In the above 'realistic' case, Greta's Gluten-Free Goodies starts with $5000 in cash but she needs to utilize some of that money to cover a loss in Net Income in the first month. In subsequent months, Greta anticipates that sales will increase as people hear of her business and the summer market gets into full swing so that by the second month of operating Greta will turn a profit and remain profitable throughout the rest of the season. It's worth noting though that Greta doesn't expect o make up from the initial cash shortfall on that first month until the end of her third month of business.

[89]

	May	June	July	Aug	Sept	Oct
Fixed Costs						
Kitchen Facilities	$ 550	$ 550	$ 550	$ 550	$ 550	$ 550
Office Supplies	$ -	$ 50	$ -	$ -	$ 50	$ -
Telephone/Internet	$ 110	$ 110	$ 110	$ 110	$ 110	$ 110
Accounting	$ 40	$ 40	$ 40	$ 40	$ 40	$ 40
Website	$ 35	$ 35	$ 35	$ 35	$ 35	$ 35
Total Monthly Fixed Costs	**$ 735**	**$ 785**	**$ 735**	**$ 735**	**$ 785**	**$ 735**
Variable Costs						
Ingredients	$ 250	$ 250	$ 300	$ 300	$ 250	$ 200
Marketing						
Farmers' Market Minimum Fee	$ 120	$ 120	$ 120	$ 120	$ 120	$ 120
Print Advertising	$ -	$ -	$ -	$ -	$ -	$ -
Online Advertising	$ 25	$ 25	$ 25	$ 25	$ 25	$ 25
Newsletter/e-newsletter	$ -	$ -	$ -	$30	$ -	$ -
Marketing Postcards	$ 150	$ -	$ -	$ -	$ -	$ -
Photography	$ 250	$ -	$ -	$ -	$ -	$ -
Samples	$ 6	$ 6	$ 6	$ 6	$ 6	$ 6
Total Variable Costs	**$ 801**	**$ 401**	**$ 451**	**$ 481**	**$ 401**	**$ 351**
Other Costs						
Packaging Costs						
Labels	$ 350	$ -	$ -	$ -	$ -	$ -
Bags	$ 200	$ -	$ -	$ -	$ -	$ -
Ribbon	$ 150	$ -	$ -	$ -	$ -	$ -
Total Other Costs	**$ 700**	**$ -**	**$ -**	**$ -**	**$ -**	**$ -**
Total Operating Costs	**$ 2,236**	**$ 1,186**	**$ 1,186**	**$ 1,216**	**$ 1,186**	**$ 1,086**
Projected Sales	**$ 700**	**$ 700**	**$ 1,000**	**$ 1,000**	**$ 800**	**$ 750**
Net Income (Sales - Costs)	**$ (1,536)**	**$ (486)**	**$ (186)**	**$ (216)**	**$ (386)**	**$ (336)**
Starting Cash On Hand	**$ 5,000**	**$ 3,464**	**$ 2,978**	**$ 2,792**	**$ 2,576**	**$ 2,190**
+ Net Income	**$ 3,464**	**$ 2,978**	**$ 2,792**	**$ 2,576**	**$ 2,190**	**$ 1,854**
Ending Cash On Hand	**$ 3,464**	**$ 2,978**	**$ 2,792**	**$ 2,576**	**$ 2,190**	**$ 1,854**

The Worst-Case Cash Forecast shows what could happen if buyers simply aren't interested in Greta's products. Before moving forward, Greta needs to ask herself if she can handle losing most of the $5,000 she will be investing in the business should the worst-case prove true.

It should be noted that if at any point in any of your projections you show a negative amount in either the Starting or Ending Cash On Hand that means the business will not have enough money to pay its obligations and additional cash will need to be injected into the business. This is important to remember if you deliver a product now and incur the costs associated with the product now but aren't paid until a future date, such as may occur if you sell products wholesale on Net Terms, as your business will have to carry those costs until payment is received. You want to be sure that your business either has enough cash or that you would be able to put cash into it to tide you over those low periods. Keep in mind that one of the major reasons small businesses fail is that they underestimate the level of capital or cash needed to startup and maintain the business.

Greta's Gluten-Free Goodies
Best-Case Cash Forecast

	May	June	July	Aug	Sept	Oct
Fixed Costs						
Kitchen Facilities	$ 550	$ 550	$ 550	$ 550	$ 550	$ 550
Office Supplies	$ -	$ 50	$ -	$ -	$ 50	$ -
Telephone/Internet	$ 110	$ 110	$ 110	$ 110	$ 110	$ 110
Accounting	$ 40	$ 40	$ 40	$ 40	$ 40	$ 40
Website	$ 35	$ 35	$ 35	$ 35	$ 35	$ 35
Total Monthly Fixed Costs	**$ 735**	**$ 785**	**$ 735**	**$ 735**	**$ 785**	**$ 735**
Variable Costs						
Ingredients	$ 250	$ 400	$ 500	$ 600	$ 600	$ 500
Marketing						
Farmers' Market Minimum Fee	$ 120	$ 180	$ 240	$ 300	$ 300	$ 240
Print Advertising	$ -	$ -	$ -	$ -	$ -	$ -
Online Advertising	$ 25	$ 25	$ 25	$ 25	$ 25	$ 25
Newsletter/e-newsletter	$ -	$ -	$ -	$30	$ -	$ -
Marketing Postcards	$ 150	$ -	$ -	$ -	$ -	$ -
Photography	$ 250	$ -	$ -	$ -	$ -	$ -
Samples	$ 6	$ 9	$ 12	$ 15	$ 15	$ 12
Total Variable Costs	**$ 801**	**$ 614**	**$ 777**	**$ 970**	**$ 940**	**$ 777**
Other Costs						
Packaging Costs						
Labels	$ 350	$ -	$ -	$ -	$ -	$ -
Bags	$ 200	$ -	$ -	$ -	$ -	$ -
Ribbon	$ 150	$ -	$ -	$ -	$ -	$ -
Total Other Costs	**$ 700**	**$ -**	**$ -**	**$ -**	**$ -**	**$ -**
Total Operating Costs	**$ 2,236**	**$ 1,399**	**$ 1,512**	**$ 1,705**	**$ 1,725**	**$ 1,512**
Projected Sales	**$ 1,500**	**$ 2,800**	**$ 3,500**	**$ 4,500**	**$ 4,500**	**$ 3,500**
Net Income (Sales - Costs)	**$ (736)**	**$ 1,401**	**$ 1,988**	**$ 2,795**	**$ 2,775**	**$ 1,988**
Starting Cash On Hand	**$ 5,000**	**$ 4,264**	**$ 5,665**	**$ 7,653**	**$ 10,448**	**$ 13,223**
+ Net Income	**$ 4,264**	**$ 5,665**	**$ 7,653**	**$ 10,448**	**$ 13,223**	**$ 15,211**
Ending Cash On Hand	**$ 4,264**	**$ 5,665**	**$ 7,653**	**$ 10,448**	**$ 13,223**	**$ 15,211**

If things go really well though, as evidenced in this Best-Case Cash Forecast, Greta could triple her investment by the end of the summer.

Note how the Variable Costs change in this case given that Greta would have to buy more ingredients and would owe more to the farmers' market association every week.

When it comes to Cash Forecasting there are certainly no guarantees, but by creating a Realistic, Best-Case, and Worst-Case scenario, you'll be able to better determine if you can handle the ups and downs of cash flow whether business is as you anticipate, better, or worse than planned.

Income Statements

A projected Income Statement (also referred to as a Profit and Loss Statement) provides you with a reality check to help determine if your business is financially sound and will be something investors and bankers will want to see if you look for funding from an outside party. Obviously, when starting up a new business, many of the figures you'll input into a projected Income Statement are estimates based on research you've done and, when in doubt, your best guess. The Income Statement should work in tandem with your 'realistic' Cash Forecast in that anticipated expenses and revenue hopefully shouldn't differ materially between the two.

Don't be alarmed if in the first year Net Income isn't as much as you anticipated. The first year for any business is a year of building and learning and you incur most of the startup expenses at that time. While for a small food business the startup costs are minimal, there are certain things, such as marketing materials and a website that you need to spend money on in Year 1 but that can be used in Year 2 and beyond. If at all possible, create projected Income Statements for the next several years to determine when exactly your business will break even and become profitable if not in the first year.

The worksheet on page 128 provides a basic guide on how to create a projected Income Statement. Once your business is up and running it is highly recommended that you purchase a business accounting software that will be able to compile all sales and expenses you enter to produce financial statements that can be used for banking and tax purposes.

Balance Sheets

Often referred to as a snapshot of a company's financial position, the Balance Sheet provides you with a picture of your business' assets, liabilities, and Net Worth at a specific point in time, for example, at month's or year end. A business' Net Worth, or owner's equity, is calculated by taking into account all assets that have monetary value whether it be cash, inventory, accounts receivable (money that is owed to the business from customers), and any equipment or real property the business may own and subtracting all liabilities or debts the business has. The difference between the Total Assets and the Total Liabilities is the Equity or Net Worth of the company.

Since a Balance Sheet highlights a company's financial health at a specific date, a projected Balance Sheet for a startup business is less critical since you will have to fill it with figures that are assumptions that may very well change before said time period occurs. While useful to a certain degree, the real benefit of a projected Balance Sheet is being able to use it if seeking outside funding for your business. After starting your business, Balance Sheets are very useful when used in combination with your Income Statement to gauge your company's financial performance. A sample projected Balance Sheet is in the Sample Business Plan on page 120 and a projected Balance Sheet Worksheet is on page 129.

A Final Note on Financials

If you're not numbers-driven the concept of Cash Forecasts, Income Statements, and Balance Sheets may seem overwhelming. However, these tools are critical in helping you decide whether your business is viable before you start and crucial in helping you keep it on a strong footing once the business is up and running. The *Money Money Money* chapter starting on page 99 goes into more detail about how to keep track of your financials but the importance of knowing how your company is doing financially cannot be stressed enough.

With the help of business accounting software like Quicken® or QuickBooks®, you will be able to keep track of your business' revenue and expenses and can easily create Income Statements and Balance Sheets with a quick click of the button. Because it is so important, you should plan to review your company's financials on a regular basis, be it daily, weekly, or monthly, and compare those results to the prior weeks, months, and years. This will help you quickly identify how your business is growing and allow you to take any remedial steps as needed. Think of this as taking the financial pulse of your business on a regular basis.

A Last Word on Business Plans

A business plan should be a living document. This means that it shouldn't be something you write up once as an exercise and then forget about on your computer or toss into the back of some drawer. After you've put all this time and energy into your plan, use it to help guide you through your first year. Since your business plan will undoubtedly change as your business changes and market conditions change, revisit your business plan at least once a year and update it to reflect where your business is and where you want it to go. Just like in the initial stages of writing the plan, sitting down with your plan annually will help you strategize how best to grow your business. Things change, and your business plan must be responsive to those changes.

How They Got Their Start
The Savory Gourmet

After more than 20 years of working as an environmental lawyer and nearing her late 50's, Marcia Newlands knew she needed a change. The firm she had been with for the past two decades was shifting its business focus away from her area of expertise and she knew she should either develop a new specialty or consider leaving the firm altogether. Feeling as though the ground had moved completely her, Marcia made an appointment with a counselor to help organize her career goals and figure out what her next steps should be. "One minute I was ready to run off and teach English in Peru and the next I was thinking I should send out resumes to other law firms," Marcia says with a smile. "The counselor helped me drill down to the very essence of what makes me happy and I realized it was cooking for other people."

Marcia spent about six months doing double-duty working as a lawyer during the day and researching every aspect of running a business at night. It reminded her of her pre-law school days, she says, when she'd work all day and would then study for the law entrance exam at night since she couldn't afford to give up her full-time job. In much the same way, Marcia went to work every day and would then come home and invest several hours a night into putting her business plan in place or taking classes with the Small Business Administration. She even used paid vacation time to take a culinary certification course with the United States Personal Chef Association. "I tried to learn everything I possibly could about running a business before I had to give up my full-time paycheck," she says.

During that time she spread the word to everyone she knew that she was available for hire for catered events on the weekends as that was the only free time she had. It turned out that several of her first clients came from her contacts in the legal world and through her connections with a local triathlon club of which she was a member.

The feedback she got from those initial events convinced her that she was on the right path so after approximately six months she left her law position, became a member of the private chef's association, and began The Savory Gourmet, a personal chef and catering business.

Though the personal chef business gave her solid experience, it didn't bring in enough revenue to support her. Being a personal chef requires a chef to offer different menus for each client family and cook those meals in the respective family's home. "I realized that the only way to really make money at it was to cook for two or more families on the same day but since everyone required separate menus, separate shopping trips, and packing and unpacking of my equipment at each home I just couldn't do it. Maybe if I was 25 I could have but I was nearing 60!" Even though Marcia was also taking catering jobs for special events, she feared her business – the mainstay of which were private chef clients – might not survive. Around that same time, a friend of Marcia's put her meal delivery business up for sale and Marcia decided to change strategy and bought the business contacts and database.

Meal delivery is different from being a personal chef in that with meal delivery you offer a weekly menu and clients choose what, if anything, they'd like. The meals are all cooked in one central kitchen and delivered to the clients' homes once a week. This enabled Marcia to start buying ingredients in bulk which cut down on her costs significantly and increased her margins. Even though she wasn't making as much on a per client basis, she could work with significantly more meal delivery clients so her business grew handsomely. Best of all, the structure of the meal delivery business meant that she only had to cook 1-2 days a week to get the orders completed and delivered. This left her plenty of time to focus on her catering business which was simultaneously growing in leaps and bounds.

"I really relied on word of mouth for marketing," Marcia says, "and the business grew organically as customers told their friends about The Savory Gourmet and they in turn told their friends." One area Marcia did put a lot of focus into was having a professional website *designed so that it fit with the look she wanted for her company. Compared to many of her competitors' websites, which appeared to have been made as cheaply as possible, Marcia wanted her website to look as good as her meals and was willing to pay an expert to build the site for her. Because part of The Savory Gourmet's mission was making people's lives easier, Marcia also had her web developer custom design a meal ordering system for the meal delivery business so that customers could easily go online and order their food for the following week with a simple click of the mouse.*

Other then the website, Marcia did little in the way of internet marketing as her business grew quickly on its own. "Looking back," Marcia says, "I wish I had invested more time and energy into internet marketing. When I started The Savory Gourmet that entire world was just beginning to be something a small business could tap into. Now it's obviously old hat and a given that your business will do some sort of internet marketing but I just felt like that was one too many new tricks for this old dog. If I could do it over I would have set aside marketing dollars for my web designer, who obviously knew what she was doing, to develop and execute an internet marketing strategy for me."

The company's explosive growth wasn't always easy to manage. In addition to doing all the shopping, menu organization, cooking, delivering, and setting up for catered events, Marcia was also doing all her own bookkeeping. Or rather, she meant to do it. At the end of her first year, with a tax filing deadline rapidly approaching and dozens of holiday parties to cater on her schedule, Marcia realized she had months of receipts sitting on her desk; none of which had been entered into her business accounting program. With her CPA breathing down her neck, Marcia managed to finish the bookkeeping entries in just enough time for her CPA to file her business taxes. Then she promptly went out and contracted a professional bookkeeper to keep her books up to date going forward. "I should have hired outside help earlier," Marcia says, "I simply did not have enough time in the day to do everything. And honestly, I started this business because I loved to cook, not because I wanted to become a bookkeeper."

Right about the time The Savory Gourmet turned five years old, Marcia decided she was ready for her next adventure. The business had supported her financially and she loved it but she was ready for something new. So she packed away her knives and sold off some of her extra kitchen equipment and then, rather then retire to a warm beach somewhere, she joined the Peace Corps for a two year assignment in North Africa. What she does upon her return is still an open question.

Funding Your Dream

It seems like every time you turn around you hear another rags-to-riches entrepreneur story about someone who started out selling lemonade on their front lawn and became the lemonade king by age twelve. What a lot of these stories neglect to tell you is how those entrepreneurs actually managed to start or grow their business since it costs money to do both those things. You may hope that one day a wealthy investor will come knocking on your door and offer to buy your company for $10 million. But for now, starting as a part-time food entrepreneur, you're likely going to have to look elsewhere for your startup funding.

First and foremost, you should complete your company's business plan and projected financials. This will give you a strong idea of how much money you'll need to get started and when you anticipate earning revenue. You will be able to approximate your cash needs and know when there might be shortfalls. Once you know how much money you need for the initial startup costs and how long before the business starts making money, the first place to look for funding is your own bank account. If you can fund your venture without a significant negative impact to your lifestyle it's best to start there. Self-funding enables you to keep full control and ownership of your company. And, truthfully, for most small part-time businesses, self-funding is the only reliable means of getting your business going. Even if you cannot fund all of the initial costs, you should be willing to fund as much of it as possible.

While startup costs for part-time food businesses are small in comparison to other food entrepreneurship ventures, 100% self-funding may not be an option for everyone in which case the following may be sources of capital:

People who believe in you personally and in what you're trying to accomplish are your best bet for securing any additional funding you may need. Even though these are people you know well, both you and they should still approach this as a business matter. Present them with your business plan and be prepared to tell them what you will give them in exchange for their investment into your business as there are several options available.

One option is to offer friends or family who make an investment in your company is a loan repayment plan. With these loans you may be able to obtain a lower interest rate and/or more flexible repayment terms than you'd be able to secure from a bank. If you are fortunate enough to negotiate a loan with little or no interest it's important to keep in mind that the IRS will still calculate imputed interest on the loan that the lender will need to include on their tax return. The IRS uses the Applicable Federal Rate (AFR), which is set by the US Treasury, to calculate the imputed interested that the lender will have to pay.

Alternatively, depending on how your company is structured, you can offer the friend or family a percentage ownership, or equity, in the business in exchange for their money.

The last option available, should you have any generous friends or family with financial means, is that the IRS currently allows anyone to gift money to you tax free for any purpose that you could use to fund your business. The IRS currently allows individuals to gift up to $13,000 and married couples who file jointly to gift up to $26,000 tax free per year. If you receive a monetary gift, you are not required to report the money on your tax return as long as the money is a true gift and is not expected to be repaid at any time.

Regardless of which option you choose, remember that you will have both a personal and business/financial relationship with these people. Be sure to choose who you would like to be 'partnered' with – temporarily in the case of a loan or permanently in the case of equity ownership – very carefully.

In the current economic climate, and for the foreseeable future, getting a bank loan for your startup business, including a business credit card, will be challenging especially given that your company has no track record of sales and therefore no guarantee of success. This doesn't mean you shouldn't try for a bank loan if you need funding for your business. Be aware that bank loans and even credit card applications are being more heavily scrutinized then ever before and your personal credit history will be critical in the decision process. Everything will depend on how well you've managed your finances and how much debt – such as student loans, car loans, mortgage, and credit cards - you're currently carrying.

If you have family members who are willing and financially able to personally guarantee a bank loan, this may be another alternative. While the bank will still study your business plan, a guarantee from a financially strong guarantor, with a good credit history, provides the bank with an independent means of repayment, should the business falter or fail.

The Small Business Administration has been tasked with trying to make more funds available to small businesses, which typically don't have ready access to traditional bank loans. The way they do this is by acting as a guarantor of the loan made through a participating financial institution. The SBA does not directly make the loan itself. While the loan application process is somewhat rigorous and you'll need to meet several SBA-required standards, an SBA loan may be the easiest way for a startup company to get funding through a bank. To learn more, visit the SBA's website at www.sba.gov which provides a wealth of information.

If you are able to secure a bank loan, whether it is backed by the SBA or not, the contract you sign will lay out a payment plan and interest that you'll be required to pay. Before signing a loan contract, build those loan payments into your business' financial projections to understand how the loan impacts your cash flow and if you can reasonably pay the loan back and operate your business based on the sales you anticipate.

Revolving Lines of Credit

In some cases it may be possible to apply for a line of credit from a bank but, again, with today's tightened lending practices this may be hard for a startup company to get without a strong personal credit history, collateral, and/or a guarantee from a financially strong family member.

Revolving lines of credit are not unlike a credit card that you can use as needed to cover business expenses and buy inventory. Lines of credit are made through a financial institution and are generally used to support seasonal working capital needs. The benefit of a line of credit over a bank loan is that you only pay interest on the money you actually use and stop paying interest once the money has been paid back. Additionally, a revolving line of credit can be used within its approved 12 month time period as working capital is needed to support the projected increases in sales. If you anticipate cash crunches where your business will need more cash then you can personally afford to invest but that can be paid back within the approved 12-month term, this type of loan may be an attractive avenue to investigate.

It is important to note, that banks generally like to see an "annual cleanup" for 30 or 60 days where the line of credit rests at zero. This proves to the bank that the line is properly structured and is only supporting temporary or seasonal working capital needs. A permanent level of working capital should not be financed by a revolving line of credit, but is more properly supported by a medium term bank loan, or preferably, funding through you own equity or private investors in exchange for equity.

Microlending

Traditionally only used in third world nations as a way to provide small amounts of startup capital to small businesses and independent entrepreneurs who can't get bank loans, the recent economic upheaval and restricted lending by banks has brought this concept to North America's shores. The idea is that even when they were lending, banks preferred to only deal with amounts greater then $50,000. As a part-time food entrepreneur this may far exceed what you want or need to take out which is where microlending can come into play. Microlending organizations disburse funds for requests that are usually less then $35,000. Like a bank, they do charge interest rates and do require that the loan be paid off in a specified timeframe. While this is still a fairly new concept to the United States, Accion USA (www.accionusa.org) is currently one of the largest microlenders to US small businesses and there are approximately 400 other microlending programs around the country.

Keeping Track of It

You want to start up a food business because you love food. But you also want to make money doing it and any money you make – or even lose – needs to be accurately accounted for. If you already have a strong grasp of your personal finances and keep track of every penny, this shouldn't be too hard for you. However, if you use the 'check what the ATM says my balance is before spending any money' method of record keeping, you'll need to spend some time devising a system that will enable you to keep track of what you spend and what you make.

If you have not done so already, you should open up a separate bank account for the business. This will help keep your personal and your business finances separate and make it easier to keep your business records straight. Once you have a business bank account set up, you should devise a recordkeeping system that will allow you to track all your expenses and all your sales. The easiest way to do this is by investing in accounting software designed for small businesses. QuickBooks® and Quicken® are two of the most popular software packages. This software helps you keep track of all of your expenses and revenue. As long as you keep it up to date, you always have an immediate snapshot of how your business is performing. In addition to helping you keep track of sales and if a client has paid on time or not, the software also takes the information you input and creates Income Statements and Balance Sheets for you.

When it comes to keeping your accounting up to date, ask yourself two questions. Are you the type of person who will be organized enough to enter all of your receipts and sales in a timely manner? If the answer is no then you have to evaluate how much you're willing to spend for a bookkeeper to do that work for you. You may find that it's worth your peace of mind to hire someone else to keep your books up to date. If you'd rather not pay for a bookkeeper, once you have a system in place it's not hard to keep your accounting books updated yourself if that's the road you choose to follow.

However, it is a good idea to hire an accountant or, at the very least, consult with one. Depending on how you've structured and registered your business there are a multitude of small tax regulations that should be taken under consideration when filing your business taxes. For example, did you know that any money you invest into your business to get it started can usually be written into the business as a loan? This means that when the business is able to repay the loan you won't be taxed on the principle loan amount repaid. As a sole proprietor, partnership, or LLC you can also usually write off any business losses on your personal income taxes. There are numerous small but crucial rules that an accountant can help you sort through to make sure that any state and federal business taxes are filed correctly and that you are taking full advantage of the available business deductions.

How I Got My Start
Petit Four Legs

My small business has taken a different path than most as it started out as part-time, became my full-time job for several years, and then went back to being part-time. I chose to include my story because the product I make is very different from the rest and also to show that once a business becomes full-time it doesn't necessarily have to stay that way.

Like most small food businesses, my business started in my own personal kitchen. Or rather, the tiny cramped apartment kitchen during my final year of graduate business school. While my classmates were dreaming of jobs on Wall Street, I was testing dog treat recipes.

Yes, you read that right – Petit Four Legs is a handcrafted dog treat company. I had started my career years earlier as a professional pastry chef for a luxury hotel chain but after several years of 14 hour days, burnt out and tired, I sought refuge in a graduate MBA program. During that time I happened to intern for a large pet food manufacturer where it became apparent to me that there was a market for high-end handmade dog treats that wasn't being met by any of the big companies. I figured this was the perfect complement to my pastry arts background so I spent much of my last year of graduate school writing a preliminary business plan and testing out recipes in my tiny kitchen while also attending school full-time.

My plan was not only to create unique handcrafted treats that mimicked the best of human treats in look while using healthy, human-grade, all-natural ingredients, but to also package the treats in a way that was reminiscent of high-end human goodies. To that end I stayed far away from anything with 'bones' on it and hired a graphic designer to create something that would stand out on retailers' shelves. Once we had a design I liked, I spent $500 to have four sample boxes created.

In what could best be described as naivety, I then sent two of those *sample boxes filled with my specialty treats to Neiman Marcus as I felt that the handcrafted aspect of the treats and the luxurious packaging would be a perfect fit for their customer demographic. Low and behold, after several weeks of worrying that I'd just blindly sent $250 worth of sample boxes out the door, they got back to me and agreed to carry my treats on their website. Signing Neiman Marcus as my first retailer gave me the confidence I needed to forgo outside employment and I decided to work on my company full-time after business school.*

I spent the next three and half years working feverishly to build the company and gain brand exposure. Everything from developing new products, working with a graphic artist to design packaging for those new products, teaching myself photo software in order to create print ads for trade publications, keeping my accounting books up-to-date, and attending industry tradeshows.

Petit Four Legs grew substantially every year. The core of the business is made up of wholesale accounts from small independent retailers throughout North America. In addition to the wholesale business, my company also has an online retail presence, and attends select craft shows and farmers' markets.

At one point, as the business grew, I thought it would be beneficial to hire a PR agency in order to garner press about my company. In what stands as the single worst business decision I ever made, I hired a firm that had extensive PR experience but no experience pitching food or pet products. Unfortunately the firm continually sent out press releases with incorrect information and conceived of PR stunts that, in my mind, degraded the brand I'd developed. During the five months I worked with them, the PR firm spent my money unsuccessfully going after high-profile press while neglecting the easy targets such as industry specific publications that are read by the retailers that make up my core customer base. I ended the relationship when I realized that I knew the industry far better than they did and could do a better job on my own. But not before I spent more than $10,000!

Over the years, as I developed new products and added them to the product portfolio, it became evident that my business had a high degree of seasonality. My dog treats became something that people gave as gifts to their dogs and dog-loving friends rather than as everyday treats. On the one hand this was fine by me. The dog treat market is crowded with competitors both large and small, and I figured that if I could carve out a little niche and become the leading treat company in the 'gifting' category then it would provide me with more than enough business. However, that also meant that the fall and winter seasons were incredibly busy as stores planned for the holidays and I found myself with limited sales and limited work in the spring and summer.

As I entered my fourth year of business I decided to use the extra time I had in the spring and summer to volunteer for a nonprofit organization. I figured that by becoming a volunteer I would not only be giving back to my community, but it would also get me out of the house and, more importantly, out of my own head as I was constantly thinking and worrying about the business. My decision to volunteer also coincided with the downturn in the economy and I realized that nothing positive would come of me sitting at home worrying about the future when the best thing I could do was just sit tight and keep a firm reign on business expenses.

Several months later a part-time position opened up at the nonprofit organization that literally seemed to have been written for me. Despite the fact I wasn't looking for a job, I felt that I had to send in a resume just to see what would happen. Next thing I knew I was called in for an interview and offered the job.

I won't lie and say I took the job without hesitation. The idea of going back to work for someone else, even if only on a part-time basis, was nerve-wracking. Most important to me was how the position would impact Petit Four Legs since that was my priority. At the same time though, with experts saying that the economic recovery might take several years, I felt that this was an opportunity to work for an organization I believed in and the money I earned could help fund my business if needed.

I worked out an agreement with the nonprofit that enables me to work more hours during the spring and summer and cut back during *the fall and winter when Petit Four Legs is busy. Little did I realize how much I would love this arrangement. The flexibility of the position enables me to work on my business and leaves me time to work in my shared commercial kitchen space. The nonprofit position provides some extra income that can be used to fund Petit Four Legs if times get tough which keeps me from worrying too much about the future of the business. My nonprofit position also gives me something positive to work on which is incredibly helpful on days when things in the dog treat world aren't going quite as planned.*

I can't say it's always been easy. There have been weeks where between orders that have to be made and shipped for Petit Four Legs and projects that have to be completed for the nonprofit organization, I feel as though I can barely keep my head above water. It's not uncommon for me to wake up before 6am and spend several hours making Petit Four Legs products or working on administrative tasks before changing clothes and heading to work. During the fall and winter it's simply a given that I will spend most weekends putting orders together for shipment the following week.

But the combination of the two jobs has, overall, been nothing but positive. Whereas I was worried that not devoting my full attention to Petit Four Legs would negatively impact the company, it turns out that the company has flourished during this time. Despite a terrible economy, the company has added new retailers and increased sales significantly. As competitors fall by the wayside, I'm confident that I'm going to be able to keep growing Petit Four Legs and that in the future I will have the option of returning to the business full-time.

Greta's Gluten-Free Goodies LLC

Business Plan

(Date)

Greta Coates
Founder & Chef
Address
Address
Phone
Email
Company Website if Applicable

Greta's Gluten-Free Goodies LLC

Greta's Gluten-Free Goodies, a registered LLC in Washington state, has a mission to provide high-quality, all-natural gluten-free baked goods. Greta Coates, the founder and chef, owns 95% of the company and her sister, Anne Coates, has 5% of the equity in exchange for Anne's investment into the Company. Based in Seattle, WA, the Company will initially, during its first season of operation, offer three products. The Company's strategy for success is based on two important criteria – a commitment to quality ingredients and offering unique products to the marketplace. Once these initial items are established in the marketplace and Greta's Gluten-Free Goodies has strong brand recognition with its core customer base, the Company plans to expand into additional products to ensure the Company's continued success.

Operating Criteria

In accordance with state and federal health codes, Greta's Gluten-Free Goodies has rented commercial kitchen space from Bryan's Baked Goods, a company that specializes in gourmet biscuits. The agreement includes up to 15 hours of kitchen time weekly in addition to full use of all bakery equipment. As an added bonus, Bryan's Baked Goods does not use wheat or gluten ingredients in any of their cooking so there is minimal risk for cross-contamination of the Company's products. The Company has been certified by King County health inspectors and Greta Jaffe, the chef and sole employee, has passed the necessary food handlers exam.

Business Risks

Greta's Goodies' biggest business risk is the potential for ingredient contamination that could undermine the flavor of the products or sicken customers. To mitigate this risk, the Company has developed relationships with local ingredient purveyors where possible and, in cases where that is not economically viable, procures ingredients from reputable vendors.

Other Business Risks Includes

Potential for liability if the products do not meet health standards or cause health issues. Loss of revenue if products do not sell as anticipated.

Insurance

The Company is currently insured for up to $1,000,000 in damages to either property, equipment, or due to any lawsuits that may be brought against it.

Current Year Business Goals

- Create a brand that is recognizable to the core target market
- Earn back all startup costs and turn a profit of $500/weekly by year-end
- *Stretch Goal: Be featured on Food Network*

Next Year's Business Goals

- Grow wholesale business to include 10 health food stores
- Increase summer farmers' market business by 33%
- *Stretch Goal: Earn enough to seriously consider buying out direct competitor Tyr's Treats*

Target Market

Greta's Gluten-Free Goodies is targeted at customers with Celiac disease who must eat a gluten-free diet for their health and those who choose to eat a gluten-free diet. In the past ten years, incidences of celiac disease in the Pacific Northwest have quadrupled and an increased focus on health has many customers cutting items that contain gluten from their diet. Customers may give up gluten but they don't necessarily want to give up many of the sweets they love, like cookies, that contain gluten. Greta's Gluten-Free Goodies is targeted to people living in and around the Seattle area who are looking for an all-natural gluten-free way to keep eating the treats they know and love. Since they understand that gluten-free cooking differs from traditional cooking, these customers are less price conscious and are willing to pay more for quality products.

Competition

The gluten-free treat market is highly fragmented with several large companies focused on the mass merchandiser and large supermarket chains, specialty bakeries that have a storefront, and small individual businesses making up the market participants. With regards to the products the Company will be offering and the target market the Company is focused on, the largest competitor appears to be Tyr's Treats, an independent business that offers a range of baked goods including a handful of gluten-free items. Tyr's Treats sells at several farmers markets throughout the area and word on the street is that they are planning to open up a mobile food truck later this year which will enable them to offer their treats at various points around the city.

Product Portfolio

Greta's Gluten-Free Goodies will initially launch with three cookies: Chocolate Inferno, Butterscotch Delight, and Mexican Wedding Cookies. All three cookies will be made by hand and made without gluten.

Sales Channels

Greta's Gluten-Free Goodies Cookies will be available weekly at the Woodland Farmers Market starting at the end of May. This market does not currently have any gluten-free vendors and the scheduling of the market, from 3-7pm on Fridays, is primetime for people who are craving a little late afternoon snack or thinking about the need to bring some treats home for the weekend. The Company has already been accepted into this farmers' market.

Greta's Gluten-Free Goodies can also be pre-ordered for special events for pickup from the market on Friday nights or for delivery on Saturdays or Sundays. Information about special events ordering will be available at the Company's farmers market booth and online on our website.

Later in the summer, after a customer base has been established, the Company plans to contact local health food stores to see if they would like to carry Greta's Gluten-Free Goodies in their stores.

Packaging

At the farmers' market, customers will have the opportunity to purchase pre-packaged bags containing three cookies or purchase individual cookies to go. Special events packaging will be a simple bakery box, tied with a ribbon and a Greta's Gluten-Free Goodies sticker as it will be the events coordinator's responsibility to showcase the cookies in the manner they best see fit. All Special Events orders will also include a business card. Packaging of this type for both sales channels will add minimal cost but the distinctive Greta's Gluten-Free Goodies label on all pre-packaged bags and special events boxes reinforces the Company's name with customers.

Pricing

At the farmers' market, cookies will be priced at $2 each or $5 for a package of three cookies. This allows the Company a healthy profit margin while also making the cookies affordably priced for farmers' market consumers.

For Special Events, cookies will be sold by the dozen for $22.

Marketing Strategy

The Company believes that the Woodland Farmers' Market will provide exposure to a wide range of customers on a weekly basis which will help drive customer awareness from a grassroots level. To further enhance awareness, the Company will hand out postcards that have pictures of the product on one side and company and ordering information on the other. From an online standpoint, the Company will have a website designed that will enable people to place orders on the site and the Company will also do some online advertising such as targeting newly engaged couples in the Seattle area through FaceBook and Google Adwords. The Company also plans to send out samples to area events planners to alert them to the product offerings and the Company is investigating whether it will be possible to purchase an ad in the local wedding magazine.

Greta's Gluten-Free Goodies
Product Cost and Pricing

Chocolate Inferno Cookies
Product Cost

Ingredients	Amount Used (ounces)	Per Unit Cost	Total
gluten-free flour	5	$ 0.30	$ 1.50
cocoa powder	0.33	$ 0.13	$ 0.04
butter	8	$ 0.04	$ 0.32
eggs (per egg)	2	$ 0.15	$ 0.30
cayenne pepper	0.12	$ 0.29	$ 0.03
Total Ingredient Cost			$ 2.19
Per Piece Product Ingredient Cost (12 pieces)			$ 0.18

Farmers' Market Packaging

Packaging	Amount Used	Per Unit Cost	Total
Labels	1	$ 0.29	$ 0.29
Bags	1	$ 0.06	$ 0.06
Total Product Packaging Cost			$ 0.35

Number of Cookies per package	3
Total Per Package Ingredient Cost	$ 0.54
Total Product Cost with Packaging	$ 0.89

Special Events

Packaging	Amount Used	Per Unit Cost	Total
Labels	1	$ 0.29	$ 0.29
Box	1	$ 0.36	$ 0.36
Ribbon	.25 yards	$1.89/yd	$ 0.47
Total Product Packaging Cost			$ 1.12

Number of Cookies per package	12
Total Per Package Ingredient Cost	$ 2.19
Total Product Cost with Packaging	$ 3.31

Product Pricing

Sales Channel	Cost	Price Charged	Profit
Farmers' Market			
Individual Cookie	$ 0.18	$ 2.00	$ 1.82
Packaged Cookies	$ 0.89	$ 5.00	$ 4.11
Special Events	$ 3.31	$22.00	$18.69

[115]

Greta's Gluten-Free Goodies
Realistic Cash Forecast

	May	June	July	Aug	Sept	Oct
Fixed Costs						
Kitchen Facilities	$ 550	$ 550	$ 550	$ 550	$ 550	$ 550
Office Supplies	$ -	$ 50	$ -	$ -	$ 50	$ -
Telephone/Internet	$ 110	$ 110	$ 110	$ 110	$ 110	$ 110
Accounting	$ 40	$ 40	$ 40	$ 40	$ 40	$ 40
Website	$ 35	$ 35	$ 35	$ 35	$ 35	$ 35
Total Monthly Fixed Costs	**$ 735**	**$ 785**	**$ 735**	**$ 735**	**$ 785**	**$ 735**
Variable Costs						
Ingredients	$ 250	$ 300	$ 350	$ 350	$ 300	$ 250
Marketing						
Farmers' Market Minimum Fee	$ 120	$ 140	$ 160	$ 160	$ 140	$ 120
Print Advertising	$ -	$ -	$ -	$ -	$ -	$ -
Online Advertising	$ 25	$ 25	$ 25	$ 25	$ 25	$ 25
Newsletter/e-newsletter	$ -	$ -	$ -	$30	$ -	$ -
Marketing Postcards	$ 150	$ -	$ -	$ -	$ -	$ -
Photography	$ 250	$ -	$ -	$ -	$ -	$ -
Samples	$ 6	$ 7	$ 8	$ 8	$ 7	$ 6
Total Variable Costs	**$ 801**	**$ 472**	**$ 543**	**$ 573**	**$ 472**	**$ 401**
Other Costs						
Packaging Costs						
Labels	$ 350	$ -	$ -	$ -	$ -	$ -
Bags	$ 200	$ -	$ -	$ -	$ -	$ -
Ribbon	$ 150	$ -	$ -	$ -	$ -	$ -
Total Other Costs	**$ 700**	**$ -**	**$ -**	**$ -**	**$ -**	**$ -**
Total Operating Costs	**$ 2,236**	**$ 1,257**	**$ 1,278**	**$ 1,308**	**$ 1,257**	**$ 1,136**
Projected Sales	**$ 1,200**	**$ 1,600**	**$ 2,000**	**$ 2,000**	**$ 1,800**	**$ 1,300**
Net Income (Sales - Costs)	**$ (1,036)**	**$ 343**	**$ 722**	**$ 692**	**$ 543**	**$ 164**
Starting Cash On Hand	**$ 5,000**	**$ 3,964**	**$ 4,307**	**$ 5,029**	**$ 5,721**	**$ 6,264**
+ Net Income	**$ 3,964**	**$ 4,307**	**$ 5,029**	**$ 5,721**	**$ 6,264**	**$ 6,428**
Ending Cash On Hand	**$ 3,964**	**$ 4,307**	**$ 5,029**	**$ 5,721**	**$ 6,264**	**$ 6,428**

Greta's Gluten-Free Goodies
Best-Case Cash Forecast

	May	June	July	Aug	Sept	Oct
Fixed Costs						
Kitchen Facilities	$ 550	$ 550	$ 550	$ 550	$ 550	$ 550
Office Supplies	$ -	$ 50	$ -	$ -	$ 50	$ -
Telephone/Internet	$ 110	$ 110	$ 110	$ 110	$ 110	$ 110
Accounting	$ 40	$ 40	$ 40	$ 40	$ 40	$ 40
Website	$ 35	$ 35	$ 35	$ 35	$ 35	$ 35
Total Monthly Fixed Costs	**$ 735**	**$ 785**	**$ 735**	**$ 735**	**$ 785**	**$ 735**
Variable Costs						
Ingredients	$ 250	$ 400	$ 500	$ 600	$ 600	$ 500
Marketing						
Farmers' Market Minimum Fee	$ 120	$ 180	$ 240	$ 300	$ 300	$ 240
Print Advertising	$ -	$ -	$ -	$ -	$ -	$ -
Online Advertising	$ 25	$ 25	$ 25	$ 25	$ 25	$ 25
Newsletter/e-newsletter	$ -	$ -	$ -	$30	$ -	$ -
Marketing Postcards	$ 150	$ -	$ -	$ -	$ -	$ -
Photography	$ 250	$ -	$ -	$ -	$ -	$ -
Samples	$ 6	$ 9	$ 12	$ 15	$ 15	$ 12
Total Variable Costs	**$ 801**	**$ 614**	**$ 777**	**$ 970**	**$ 940**	**$ 777**
Other Costs						
Packaging Costs						
Labels	$ 350	$ -	$ -	$ -	$ -	$ -
Bags	$ 200	$ -	$ -	$ -	$ -	$ -
Ribbon	$ 150	$ -	$ -	$ -	$ -	$ -
Total Other Costs	**$ 700**	**$ -**	**$ -**	**$ -**	**$ -**	**$ -**
Total Operating Costs	**$ 2,236**	**$ 1,399**	**$ 1,512**	**$ 1,705**	**$ 1,725**	**$ 1,512**
Projected Sales	**$ 1,500**	**$ 2,800**	**$ 3,500**	**$ 4,500**	**$ 4,500**	**$ 3,500**
Net Income (Sales - Costs)	**$ (736)**	**$ 1,401**	**$ 1,988**	**$ 2,795**	**$ 2,775**	**$ 1,988**
Starting Cash On Hand	**$ 5,000**	**$ 4,264**	**$ 5,665**	**$ 7,653**	**$ 10,448**	**$ 13,223**
+ Net Income	**$ 4,264**	**$ 5,665**	**$ 7,653**	**$ 10,448**	**$ 13,223**	**$ 15,211**
Ending Cash On Hand	**$ 4,264**	**$ 5,665**	**$ 7,653**	**$ 10,448**	**$ 13,223**	**$ 15,211**

[117]

Greta's Gluten-Free Goodies
Worst-Case Cash Forecast

	May	June	July	Aug	Sept	Oct
Fixed Costs						
Kitchen Facilities	$ 550	$ 550	$ 550	$ 550	$ 550	$ 550
Office Supplies	$ -	$ 50	$ -	$ -	$ 50	$ -
Telephone/Internet	$ 110	$ 110	$ 110	$ 110	$ 110	$ 110
Accounting	$ 40	$ 40	$ 40	$ 40	$ 40	$ 40
Website	$ 35	$ 35	$ 35	$ 35	$ 35	$ 35
Total Monthly Fixed Costs	**$ 735**	**$ 785**	**$ 735**	**$ 735**	**$ 785**	**$ 735**
Variable Costs						
Ingredients	$ 250	$ 250	$ 300	$ 300	$ 250	$ 200
Marketing						
Farmers' Market Minimum Fee	$ 120	$ 120	$ 120	$ 120	$ 120	$ 120
Print Advertising	$ -	$ -	$ -	$ -	$ -	$ -
Online Advertising	$ 25	$ 25	$ 25	$ 25	$ 25	$ 25
Newsletter/e-newsletter	$ -	$ -	$ -	$30	$ -	$ -
Marketing Postcards	$ 150	$ -	$ -	$ -	$ -	$ -
Photography	$ 250	$ -	$ -	$ -	$ -	$ -
Samples	$ 6	$ 6	$ 6	$ 6	$ 6	$ 6
Total Variable Costs	**$ 801**	**$ 401**	**$ 451**	**$ 481**	**$ 401**	**$ 351**
Other Costs						
Packaging Costs						
Labels	$ 350	$ -	$ -	$ -	$ -	$ -
Bags	$ 200	$ -	$ -	$ -	$ -	$ -
Ribbon	$ 150	$ -	$ -	$ -	$ -	$ -
Total Other Costs	**$ 700**	**$ -**	**$ -**	**$ -**	**$ -**	**$ -**
Total Operating Costs	**$ 2,236**	**$ 1,186**	**$ 1,186**	**$ 1,216**	**$ 1,186**	**$ 1,086**
Projected Sales	**$ 700**	**$ 700**	**$ 1,000**	**$ 1,000**	**$ 800**	**$ 750**
Net Income (Sales - Costs)	**$ (1,536)**	**$ (486)**	**$ (186)**	**$ (216)**	**$ (386)**	**$ (336)**
Starting Cash On Hand	$ 5,000	$ 3,464	$ 2,978	$ 2,792	$ 2,576	$ 2,190
+ Net Income	$ 3,464	$ 2,978	$ 2,792	$ 2,576	$ 2,190	$ 1,854
Ending Cash On Hand	$ 3,464	$ 2,978	$ 2,792	$ 2,576	$ 2,190	$ 1,854

Greta's Gluten-Free Goodies LLC
Projected Income Statement (Realistic Case)
May 1 - October 30 Year 1

	Total
Income	
Sales	9,968.90
Special Events Delivery Fees	171.64
Total Income	$ 9,968.90
Cost of Goods Sold	
Food Supplies	1,227.23
Packaging	416.04
Labor (Production)	0.00
Total Cost of Goods Sold	$ 1,643.27
Gross Profit	$ 8,325.63
Expenses	
Bank Charges	116.59
Merchant Acccount Charges	266.93
Total Bank Charges	$ 383.52
Business Licenses	59.00
Health Department Licenses	67.50
Total Business Licenses	$ 126.50
Legal & Professional Fees	
Accounting	240.00
Total Legal & Professional Fees	$ 240.00
Marketing	
Postcards/Business Cards/Collateral	234.87
EMarketing	169.36
Total Marketing	$ 404.23
Office Expenses	$ 201.38
Rent or Lease	$ 3,300.00
Labor (Administrative)	$ -
Sales Generation	
Farmers Market Booth Fees	900.00
Craft Show Booth Fee	200.00
Total Sales Generation	$ 1,100.00
Total Expenses	$ 5,755.63
Net Income	**$ 2,570.00**

Greta's Gluten-Free Goodies LLC
Projected Balance Sheet (Realistic Case)
6 Months Ending Oct 30 Year 1

	Total
ASSETS	
Current Assets	
Bank Accounts	
Greta's Business Bank Account	5,028.00
Total Bank Accounts	$ 5,028.00
Other Current Assets	
Packaging Inventory	167.00
Total Other Current Assets	$ 167.00
Total Current Assets	$ 5,195.00
TOTAL ASSETS	$ 5,195.00
LIABILITIES AND EQUITY	
Liabilities	
Current Liabilities	
Credit Cards	
Greta's Business Credit Card	91.71
Total Credit Cards	$ 91.71
Other Current Liabilities	
Sales tax payable	368.75
Greta Personal Loan to Business	1,164.54
Total Other Current Liabilities	$ 1,533.29
Total Current Liabilities	$ 1,625.00
Total Liabilities	$ 1,625.00
Equity	
Partner's 1 Equity--Greta	
Partner 1 Investment	950.00
Total Partner's 1 Equity--Greta	$ 950.00
Partner's 2 Equity--Greta's Sister	
Partner 2 Investment	50.00
Total Partner's 2 Equity--Greta's Sister	$ 50.00
Net Income	2,570.00
Total Equity	$ 3,570.00
TOTAL LIABILITIES AND EQUITY	$ 5,195.00

[120]

APPENDIX II
USEFUL CULINARY MEASUREMENTS & ABBREVIATIONS

Useful American Standard Cooking Measurements:

16 ounces	=	1 pound
1 cup	=	8 fluid ounces
16 fluid ounces	=	1 pint
32 fluid ounces	=	1 quart
128 fluid ounces	=	1 gallon

Common American Standard Measurement Abbreviations

tsp (or just t)	=	teaspoon
Tbl (or just T)	=	tablespoon
oz	=	ounces
lb	=	pound
pt	=	pint
qt	=	quart
gal	=	gallon

RECIPE TESTING WORKSHEET

Recipe Name
# of Servings
Date:

Weight	Ingredient

Instructions

Storage Requirements

Comments/Feedback

APPENDIX IV
PRODUCT COST WORKSHEET

[Company Name]
Product Cost

[Product Name]

Step 1A: Ingredient Unit Cost

Ingredients	Total Units Bought (total weight)	Total Price	Unit Cost

Divide Total Price by Total Units Bought to get Unit Cost

Step 1B: Product Ingredient Cost

Ingredient	Amount Used	Unit Cost	Ingredient Unit Cost

Multiply Amount Used by Unit Cost to get Ingredient Unit Cost

Step 1C: Total Ingredient Cost

Total Ingredient Cost	

Add all Ingredient Unit Costs together

Step 1D: Per Piece Ingredient Cost

Total Ingredient Cost	Number of Units Recipe Yields	Per Piece Ingredient Cost

Divide Total Ingredient Cost by Number of Units Recipe Yields

[123]

Step 2: Packaging Unit Cost

Packaging	Total Amount Bought	Total Price	Unit Cost

Divide Total Price by Total Amount Bought to get Unit Cost

Total Packaging Cost			

Mutiply each Unit Cost by the number of units used per sale

Step 3: Total Product Cost

Total Ingredient Cost (Ingredient Cost x number of products per package)	
Add in Total Packaging Cost	
Total Product Cost	

[Company Name]
Product Pricing

[Product Name]
Total Product Cost: (from Product Cost Worksheet)

Step 1: Base Price

Wholesale Price	(Total Product Cost x 2)
Retail Price	(Total Product Cost x 4)

Step 2: Adjusted Price

Adjusted Wholesale Price

Adjusted Retail Price

Adjust the price accordingly to account for specific market conditions and if product is especially time consuming.
This will be the price you sell your products for.

Step 3: Gross Profit
Gross Profit shows you how much money you will make on each product sale after you account for the costs associated with that product

Wholesale Gross Profit

Subtract the Total Product Cost from the Adjusted Wholesale Price to calculate your Wholesale Profit

Retail Gross Profit

Subtract the Total Product Cost from the Adjusted Retail Price to calculate your Wholesale Profit

Step 4: Markup
Markup is the percentage difference between the Total Product Cost and the Adjusted Wholesale/Retail Price. In some instances you may decide that you want to price a product based on the markup you would receive.

Step 4a: Calculating Markup with Price in Place

Wholesale Markup

Divide Wholesale Gross Profit by the Total Product Cost

Retail Markup

Divide Retail Gross Profit by the Total Product Cost

Step 4b: Calculating Price Based on Desired Markup
Markup Percentage You Want

Subtract Markup Percentage (in decimal form) from 1
ie - 60% = .6 = 1-.6 = .4

Divide Total Product Cost by 1-markup percentage
for Wholesale Price

Reminder - your Wholesale Markup and Retail Markup will be different from one another and should be calculated seperately

Step 5: Margin
Margin is the percentage difference between the Adjusted Price and the Gross Profit

Wholesale Margin

Divide Wholesale Gross Profit by Adjusted Wholesale Price

Retail Margin

Divide Retail Gross Profit by Adjusted Retail Price

CASH FORECAST WORKSHEET

Company Name
[Best/Realistic/Worst] Cash Forecast

Month:

Fixed Costs

Kitchen Facilities						
Office Supplies						
Telephone/Internet						
Accounting						
Website						
Add Each Month's Fixed Costs						

Variable Costs

Ingredients						
Marketing						
Add Each Month's Variable Costs						

Other Costs

Packaging Costs						
Add Each Month's Other Costs						

Add Fixed, Variable, & Other Costs						

Projected Sales						

Net Income (Sales - Costs)						

Starting Cash On Hand						
+ Net Income						
Net Income = Ending Cash						

APPENDIX VII
PROJECTED INCOME STATEMENT WORKSHEET

Your projected Income Statement line items may vary depending on the specifics of your business.

Company Name
Projected Income Statement
Date & Year

	Total
Income	
Sales	All anticipated sales (price times quantity)
Other Income	May include shipping fees, delivery fees, etc. for which you are paid
Total Income	**Add together above amounts**
Cost of Goods Sold	
Food Supplies	All anticipated ingredient costs
Packaging	All anticipated packaging costs
Labor (Production)	All labor costs attributable to cooking or packaging
Total Cost of Goods Sold	**Add together Food, Packaging, and Production Labor costs**
Gross Profit	**Total Income - Total Cost of Goods Sold**
Expenses	
Bank Charges	All anticipated bank fees except merchant or other misc fees
Merchant Acccount Charges	All anticipated merchant account fees
Other Bank Charges	All other anticipated bank fees
Total Bank Charges	**Add together all Bank, Merchant, and Other charges**
Business Licenses	All anticipated business licensing costs
Health Department Licenses	Health Department and Food Handlers fees as applicable
Total Business Licenses	**Add together all Business Licensing and Health Fees**
Legal & Professional Fees	
Accounting	All anticipated accountant, bookkeeper, or software program costs
Legal Fees	Any anticipated attorney costs
Total Legal & Professional Fees	**Add together Legal & Professional Fees**
Marketing	
Postcards/Business Cards/Collateral	Estimated or budgeted marketing collateral costs
Print Marketing	Estimated or budgeted print marketing costs
EMarketing	Estimated or budgeted eMarketing costs
Total Marketing	**Add together all Marketing expenses**
Office Expenses	May include phone, paper, etc
Rent or Lease	Kitchen rent and any other leased property or equipment
Labor (Administrative)	All labor costs not directly attributable to production
Sales Generation	Estimated expenditure will depend on sales channel
Total Expenses	**Total Sales Generation + Labor + Rent + Office + Marketing + Legal/Professional + Licenses + Bank Fees**
Net Operating Income	**Gross Profit - Total Expenses**

PROJECTED BALANCE SHEET WORKSHEET

Your projected Balance Sheet line items may vary depending on the specifics of your business.

Company name
Projected Balance Sheet
Date Year 1

	Total
ASSETS	
Current Assets	
Bank Accounts	Taken from Realistic Cash Forecast
Accounts Receivable	Anticipated outstanding revenue from sales not yet collected
Other Current Assets	
Inventory	Anticipated remaining food or packaging inventory
Total Current Assets	Add together all Current Assets
Fixed Assets	
Property/Equipement/Vehicles	Value of Fixed Assets minus accumulated depreciation
Total Fixed Assets	Add together all Fixed Assets
TOTAL ASSETS	Sum of all Current and Fixed Assets
LIABILITIES AND EQUITY	
Liabilities	
Current Liabilities	List all anticipated current liabilities - ie credit cards
Other Current Liabilities	List all other current liabilities such as taxes and loans
Total Current Liabilities	Add together all Current and Other Current Liabilities
Long-Term Liabilities	List all anticipated Long Term Liabilities like bank notes payable
Total Long-Term Liabilities	Add together all Long-Term Liabilities
TOTAL LIABILITIES	Sum of Current Liabilities and any Long-Term Liabilities
EQUITY	
Owner's Equity	Add together investments made into the business by Owner 1
Add more lines for additional Owners	
Net Income/Loss	Taken from Projected Income Statement
TOTAL EQUITY	All Partners' Equity + Retained Earnings + Net Income/Loss
TOTAL LIABILITIES AND EQUITY	Total Liabilities + Total Equity

Total Liabilities and Equity must equal Total Assets

APPENDIX IX
CULINARY RESOURCES

While by no means a comprehensive list, the following section provides respected resources for some of your culinary needs.

Ingredient Suppliers

When starting out, especially while testing recipes, it may be easiest to simply purchase ingredients at your local grocery store or supermarket. Don't forget to check with local farmers who may be willing to offer wholesale prices on their ingredients to food businesses. For ingredients you can't source locally or for larger quantities several options include:

Costco® - A members warehouse store that sells ingredients in larger quantity sizes at a discount over local grocery stores and supermarkets. (costco.com)

GloryBee Foods® - What started as a honey company has turned into a purveyor of natural foods. Call to set up a wholesale account in order to take advantage of their bulk pricing. (glorybeefoods.com)

Peterson® - While based in the Northwest with a focus on serving Northwest companies, Peterson does sell and distribute its specialty food items such as imported cheeses and hard-to-find baking and cooking ingredients nationwide. (petersoncheese.com)

Sam's Club® – Another members warehouse store selling ingredients in larger quantity sizes. (samsclub.com)

United Natural Foods, Inc ® – A respected distributor of natural and organic ingredients, produce, and culinary products. You will need to set up a wholesale account before placing orders. (unfi.com)

Packaging Suppliers

Local cake and craft stores are a great place to purchase small quantities of packaging supplies. When you're ready for larger quantities of packaging the following companies offer a wide range of options and several can do custom work as needed. Keep in mind that food packaging must meet FDA requirements for direct food contact.

Bags & Bows® - This company mainly focuses on packaging products retailers need such as shopping bags and tissue paper but also has a wide range of ribbons and shipping supplies. (bagsandbowsonline.com)

Brpboxshop® - For bakery businesses specifically, this company has numerous packaging options including several eco-friendly choices. (brpboxshop.com)

GlerupRevere Packaging® - Whether you're looking for attractive boxes, candy pads, or custom-designed labels, GlerupRevere offers just about anything a small food business needs to get started. (glerup.com)

Label Impressions® - This California based company produces a line of eco-friendly labels and can do print runs as low as 500 labels though greater discounts do apply for larger quantity orders. (labelimpressions.com)

Nashville Wraps® - This company has an extensive line of gift and food packaging products whether you're looking for ribbons, bags, or beautiful boxes. Low order minimums make this a great option for small food entrepreneurs. (nashvillewraps.com)

Papermart® - With an extensive range of products – everything from bags to boxes to ribbons to bows – this company is a great resource for small food businesses and offers very competitive prices and low minimum orders. (papermart.com)

Uline® - If you need shipping supplies such as cardboard shipping boxes or packing material, Uline is one of the largest online retailers with prices that are significantly cheaper then you will find at your local shipping store. (uline.com)

Wilton® - With its products in craft stores around the country, Wilton has a range of packaging options. Prices may be higher then you'd find through other retailers but the fact that their products are sold in small quantities makes this an ideal place to start when initially looking for packaging. (wilton.com)

Kitchen Equipment

Many cities have restaurant supply stores or even a section of the city known as 'restaurant row' where you will be able to find commercial restaurant equipment at prices lower then typical kitchen retail stores. Also be sure to keep an eye on Craigslist® where good deals can be found on used kitchen equipment. You may also want to check out your local Target®, Kmart®, or other large retailer. Depending on what piece of equipment or cooking utensil you're looking for, their prices can be very competitive. Some other places to check include:

Chef's Catalog® - Based in Colorado, Chef's Catalog is a print and online catalog mainly focused on home cooks with a wide range of cooking and baking supplies. (chefscatalog.com)

Sur La Table® - The focus of this company is to provide everything home cooks need including appliances, cookbooks, and even culinary classes. (surlatable.com)

Williams Sonoma® - Undoubtedly the powerhouse in the culinary equipment world, Williams Sonoma offers thousands of products from around the world online and in their stores. (williams-sonoma.com)

Wilton® - This company focuses on kitchen equipment for baked goods such as cake pans, piping bags, and piping tips. Many of their products can be found in craft stores or through their online store. (wilton.com)

APPENDIX X
BUSINESS RESOURCES

The following is a list of business resources and websites that have been mentioned throughout this book.

Accion USA – accionusa.org

Applicable Federal Rate – irs.gov/app/picklist/list/federalrates.html

Blogger – blogger.com

CompuFood Analysis, Inc – compufoodanalysis.com

CostCo – costco.com

Etsy – etsy.com

FaceBook – facebook.com

Foodzie – foodzie.com

GoDaddy – godaddy.com

Google Adwords – google.com/adwords

Internal Revenue Service – irs.gov

Intuit – intuit.com

NASFT Fancy Food Shows – specialtyfood.com

PayPal – paypal.com

QuickBooks – quickbooks.intuit.com

Quicken – quicken.intuit.com

Small Business Administration – sba.gov

US Patent and Trademark Office – uspto.gov

WordPress – wordpress.com

___ Build Business Plan
    ___ Business description (company description, who is your target market, who are the competitors)
    ___ Recipe testing & product cost analysis
    ___ Finalize product portfolio and pricing
    ___ Complete projected cash forecasts and financial models
    ___ Determine business structure (with legal counsel as needed)
    ___ Decide on Business Name
    ___ Outline best sales channels
    ___ Create marketing and branding strategy
___ Begin identifying outside funding sources (as needed)
___ Find kitchen space
___ Register business with state authorities
___ Register business with city or county (as needed)
___ Sign up for Employer Identification Number (as needed)
___ Register with state tax authorities
___ Pass Food Handler's Safety exam (as needed)
___ Register business with local Health authorities (as needed)
___ Open business bank accounts
___ Finalize outside funding (as needed)
___ Develop brand logo, website, and other marketing collateral
___ Purchase and familiarize yourself with accounting software
___ Register for merchant account (as needed)
___ Start sales channel logistics (signing up for farmers' markets, talk with wholesale buyers, etc)
___ Start selling!
___ Keep accounting books up to date
___ Regularly update business plan to reflect actual sales experience

APPENDIX XII
STATE AND US TERRITORY STARTUP ROADMAP

Each state and US territory provides information online about how to open a small business in that region. The following pages provide links to those government resources to help get you started. Since the rules and guidellnes for each state and US territory differ from one another, please take some time to thoroughly review the information. When in doubt, consult with an experienced business attorney or small business administration official.

IRS Employer Identification Number (EIN)   irs.gov/businesses/small/index.html

Alabama

Alabama State Website	alabama.gov
Information on Starting a Business	alabama.gov/portal/secondary.jsp?page=Business
Business Structure Filing	sos.state.al.us/BusinessServices/Default.aspx
Business Name Registration	Not necessary but can be done through Secretary of State
City or County Buiness Licensing	Contact your city or county revenue department
Business Tax Registration	ador.state.al.us/bus.html
Health Code Requirements and Permits	Contact your city or county health department
Small Business Administration Office	sba.gov/localresources/district/al/index.html

Alaska

Alaska State Website	alaska.gov
Information on Starting a Business	alaska.gov/businessHome.html
Business Structure Filing	commerce.state.ak.us/occ/cforms.htm
Business Name Registration	commerce.state.ak.us/occ/register.html
Business Tax Registration	tax.alaska.gov
Health Code Rquirements and Permits	Contact you city or county health department
Small Business Administration Office	sba.gov/localresources/district/ak/index.html

Arizona

Arizona State Website	az.gov
Information on Starting a Business	azcommerce.com/BusAsst/SmallBiz/
Business Structure Filing	azcc.gov/divisions/corporations/filings/forms/index.htm
Business Name Registration	Not necessary but can be done through Secretary of State
Business Tax Registration	aztaxes.gov
City or County Business Licenses	Contact your city or county revenue department
Health Code Requirements and Permits	Contact your city or county health department
Small Business Administration Office	sba.gov/localresources/district/ar/index.html

Arkansas

Arkansas State Website	portal.arkansas.gov
Information on Starting a Business	portal.arkansas.gov/business/Pages/default.aspx
Business Structure Filing	sos.arkansas.gov/corp_ucc_business.html
Business Name Registration	sos.arkansas.gov/corp_ucc_business.html
Business Tax Registration	dfa.arkansas.gov/offices/incomeTax/Pages/default.aspx
City or County Business Licenses	Contact you city or county health department
Health Code Requirements and Permits	Contact your city or county health department
Small Business Administration Office	sba.gov/localresources/district/ar/index.html

California

CaliforniaState Website	ca.gov
Information on Starting a Business	calbusiness.ca.gov
Business Structure Filing	sos.ca.gov/business/be/forms.htm
Business Name Registration	Contact your County Recorder Clerk's Office
Business Tax Registration	taxes.ca.gov
City or County Business Licenses	Contact your city or county revenue department
Health Code Requirements and Permits	Contact your city or county health department
Small Business Administration Office	sba.gov/localresources/district/ca/

Colorado

Colorado State Website	colorado.gov
Information on Starting a Business	colorado.gov
Business Structure Filing	sos.state.co.us/pubs/business/main.htm
Business Name Registration	sos.state.co.us/biz/FileDoc.do
Business Tax Registration	colorado.gov/revenue/tax
City or County Business Licenses	Contact your city or county revenue department
Health Code Requirements and Permits	Contact your city or county health department
Small Business Administration Office	sba.gov/localresources/district/co/index.html

Connecticut

Connecticut State Website	ct.gov
Information on Starting a Business	ct.gov/ctportal/taxonomy/taxonomy.asp?DLN=27187&ctportalNav=|27187|
Business Structure Filing	ct.gov/sots/site/default.asp
Business Name Registration	ct.gov/sots/site/default.asp
Business Tax Registration	ct.gov/drs/cwp/view.asp?a=1433&q=265880
City or County Business Licenses	Contact your city or county revenue department
Health Code Requirements and Permits	Contact your city or county health department
Small Business Administration Office	sba.gov/localresources/district/ct/index.html

Delaware

Delaware State Website	delaware.gov
Information on Starting a Business	dedo.delaware.gov
Business Structure Filing	corp.delaware.gov/howtoform.shtml
Business Name Registration	Depends on business structure
Business Tax Registration	onestop.delaware.gov/osbrlpublic/Home.jsp
City or County Business Licenses	Contact your city or county revenue department
Health Code Requirements and Permits	Contact your city or county health department
Small Business Administration Office	sba.gov/localresources/district/de/index.html

District of Columbia

District of Columbia Website	dc.gov
Information on Starting a Business	brc.dc.gov
Business Structure Filing	dcra.dc.gov/DC/DCRA/
Business Name Registration	dcra.dc.gov/DC/DCRA/
Business Tax Registration	taxpayerservicecenter.com/fr500/
Health Code Requirements and Permits	dchealth.dc.gov
Small Business Administration Office	sba.gov/localresources/district/dc/index.html

Florida

Florida State Website	myflorida.com
Information on Starting a Business	myflorida.com/taxonomy/business/
Business Structure Filing	sunbiz.org
Business Name Registration	efile.sunbiz.org/ficregintro.html
Business Tax Registration	dor.myflorida.com/dor/taxes/registration.html
City or County Business Licenses	Contact your city or county revenue department
Health Code Requirements and Permits	Contact your city or county health department
Small Business Administration Office	sba.gov/localresources/district/fl/

Georgia

Georgia State Website	georgia.gov
Information on Starting a Business	georgia.gov/00/channel_title/0,2094,4802_4971,00.html
Business Structure Filing	sos.georgia.gov/corporations/
Business Name Registration	Depends on business structure
Business Tax Registration	etax.dor.ga.gov/ctr/formsreg.aspx
City or County Business Licenses	Contact your city or county revenue department
Health Code Requirements and Permits	Contact your city or county health department
Small Business Administration Office	sba.gov/localresources/district/ga/index.html

Guam

Guam Government Website	guam.gov
Information on Starting a Business	investguam.com
Business Structure Filing	govguamdocs.com/revtax/index_revtax.htm
Business Name Registration	guamcourts.org/CompilerofLaws/GCA/18gca/18gc026.PDF
Business Tax Registration	guamtax.com/
City or County Business Licenses	Contact your city or county revenue department
Health Code Requirements and Permits	Contact Department of Health fo rmore information
Small Business Administration Office	sba.gov/localresources/district/gu/index.html

Hawaii

Hawaii State Website	hawaii.gov
Information on Starting a Business	hbe.ehawaii.gov/BizEx/home.eb
Business Structure Filing	hbe.ehawaii.gov/BizEx/home.eb
Business License Registration	hbe.ehawaii.gov/BizEx/home.eb
Business Name Registration	hbe.ehawaii.gov/BizEx/home.eb
Business Tax Registration	hbe.ehawaii.gov/BizEx/home.eb
City or County Business Licenses	Contact your city or county revenue department
Health Code Requirements and Permits	Contact your city or county health department
Small Business Administration Office	sba.gov/localresources/district/hi/index.html

Idaho

Idaho State Website	idaho.gov
Information on Starting a Business	business.idaho.gov
Business Structure Filing	sos.idaho.gov/corp/corindex.htm
Business Name Registration	sos.idaho.gov/corp/ABNform.htm
Business Tax Registration	labor.idaho.gov/applications/ibrs/ibr.aspx
City or County Business Licenses	Contact your city or county revenue department
Health Code Requirements and Permits	Contact your city or county health department
Small Business Administration Office	sba.gov/localresources/district/id/index.html

Illinois

Illinois State Website	illinois.gov
Information on Starting a Business	business.illinois.gov
Business Structure Filing	business.illinois.gov/registration.cfm
Business Name Registration	Depends on structure - cyberdriveillinois.com/
Business Tax Registration	business.illinois.gov/registration.cfm
City or County Business Licenses	Contact your city or county health department
Health Code Requirements and Permits	Contact your city or county health department
Small Business Administration Office	sba.gov/localresources/district/il/index.html

Indiana

Indiana State Website	in.gov
Information on Starting a Business	in.gov/ai/business
Business Structure Filing	in.gov/sos/business/2381.htm
Business Name Registration	File with County Recorder and in.gov/sos/business/2436.htm
Business Tax Registration	in.gov/dor/3963.htm
City or County Business Licenses	Contact your city or county revenue department
Health Code Requirements and Permits	Contact your city or county health department
Small Business Administration Office	sba.gov/localresources/district/in/index.html

Iowa

Iowa State Website	iowa.gov
Information on Starting a Business	iowa.gov/Business_and_Economic_Development
Business Structure Filing	sos.state.ia.us/business/
Business Name Registration	Either County Recorder or sos.state.ia.us/business/index.html
Business Tax Registration	idr.iowa.gov/CBA/start.asp
City or County Business Licenses	Contact your city or county revenue department
Health Code Requirements and Permits	Contact your city or county health department
Small Business Administration Office	sba.gov/localresources/district/ia

Kansas

Kansas State Website	kansas.gov
Information on Starting a Business	kansas.gov/business
Business Structure Filing	kssos.org/
Business Name Registration	kssos.org/
Business Tax Registration	ksrevenue.org/busregistration.htm
City or County Business Licenses	Contact your city or county revenue department
Health Code Requirements and Permits	Contact your city or county health department
Small Business Administration Office	sba.gov/localresources/district/ks

Kentucky

Kentucky State Website	kentucky.gov
Information on Starting a Business	kentucky.gov/business
Business Structure Filing	sos.ky.gov/business/filings/
Business Name Registration	sos.ky.gov/business/filings/
Business Tax Registration	revenue.ky.gov/business/register.htm
City or County Business Licenses	Contact your city or county revenue department
Health Code Requirements and Permits	Contact your city or county health department
Small Business Administration Office	sba.gov/localresources/district/ky/index.html

Louisiana

Louisiana State Website	louisiana.gov
Information on Starting a Business	louisiana.gov/business
Business Structure Filing	sos.louisiana.gov
Business Name Registration	Either Parish Clerk or sos.louisiana.gov
Business Tax Registration	revenue.louisiana.gov/sections/business/intro.aspx
City or County Business Licenses	Contact your city or county revenue department
Health Code Requirements and Permits	Contact your city or county health department
Small Business Administration Office	sba.gov/localresources/district/la/index.html

Maine

Maine State Website	maine.gov
Information on Starting a Business	maine.gov/portal/business/
Business Structure Filing	maine.gov/sos/cec/corp/index/html
Business Name Registration	maine.gov/sos/cec/corp/index/html
Business Tax Registration	https://www.maine.gov/online/suwtaxreg/
City or County Business Licenses	Contact your city or county revenue department
Health Code Requirements and Permits	Contact your city or county health department
Small Business Administration Office	sba.gov/localresources/district/me/index.html

Maryland

Maryland State Website	maryland.gov
Information on Starting a Business	dat.state.md.us/sdatweb/checklist.html
Business Structure Filing	dat.state.md.us/sdatweb/sdatforms.html#entity
Business Name Registration	dat.state.md.us/sdatweb/nameappl.pdf
Business Tax Registration	interactive.marylandtaxes.com/webapps/comptrollercra/entrance.asp
City or County Business Licenses	Contact your city or county revenue department
Health Code Requirements and Permits	Contact your city or county health department
Small Business Administration Office	sba.gov/localresources/district/md/index.html

Massachusetts

Massachusetts State Website	mass.gov
Information on Starting a Business	mass.gov
Business Structure Filing	sec.state.ma.us/cor/coridx.htm
Business Name Registration	Register with city or town you are doing business in
Business Tax Registration	mass.gov/?pageID=dorhomepage&L=1&L0=Home&sid=Ador
City or County Business Licenses	Contact your city or county revenue department
Health Code Requirements and Permits	Contact your city or county health department
Small Business Administration Office	sba.gov/localresources/district/ma/index.html

Michigan

Michigan State Website	michigan.gov
Information on Starting a Business	michigan.gov/som/0,1607,7-192-29943---,00.html
Business Structure Filing	michigan.gov/som/0,1607,7-192-29943---,00.html
Business Name Registration	Depends on business structure - michigan.gov/sos
Business Tax Registration	michigan.gov/0,1607,7-118--89978--,00.html
City or County Business Licenses	Contact your city or county revenue department
Health Code Requirements and Permits	Contact your city or county health department
Small Business Administration Office	sba.gov/localresources/district/mi/index.html

Minnesota

Minnesota State Website	state.mn.us
Information on Starting a Business	state.mn.us
Business Structure Filing	sos.state.mn.us/index.aspx?page=18
Business Name Registration	sos.state.mn.us/index.aspx?page=180
Business Tax Registration	mndor.state.mn.us/tp/MN_xwTapReg.aspx
City or County Business Licenses	Contact your city or county revenue department
Health Code Requirements and Permits	Contact your city or county health department
Small Business Administration Office	sba.gov/localresources/district/mn/index.html

Mississippi

Mississippi State Website	mississippi.gov
Information on Starting a Business	ms.gov/ms_sub_template.jsp?Category_ID=3
Business Structure Filing	sos.ms.gov/business_services_business_formation.aspx
Business Name Registration	Not required to register business name
Business Tax Registration	tax.ms.gov/regist.html
City or County Business Licenses	Contact your city or county revenue department
Health Code Requirements and Permits	Contact your city or county health department
Small Business Administration Office	sba.gov/localresources/district/ms/index.html

Missouri

Missouri State Website	mo.gov
Information on Starting a Business	business.mo.gov/
Business Structure Filing	sos.mo.gov/business/corporations/startBusiness.asp
Business Name Registration	sos.mo.gov/
Business Tax Registration	dor.mo.gov/business/register/
City or County Business Licenses	Contact your city or county revenue department
Health Code Requirements and Permits	Contact your city or county health department
Small Business Administration Office	sba.gov/localresources/district/mo/

Montana

Montana State Website	mt.gov
Information on Starting a Business	mt.gov/business.asp
Business Structure Filing	sos.mt.gov/Business/index.asp
Business Name Registration	sos.mt.gov/Business/index.asp
Business Tax Registration	app.mt.gov/bustax/
City or County Business Licenses	Contact your city or county revenue department
Health Code Requirements and Permits	Contact your city or county health department
Small Business Administration Office	sba.gov/localresources/district/mt/index.html

Nebraska

Nebraska State Website	nebraska.gov
Information on Starting a Business	nebraska.gov/dynamicindex.html#
Business Structure Filing	sos.ne.gov/business/corp_serv/corp_stat_menu.html
Business Name Registration	sos.ne.gov
Business Tax Registration	revenue.state.ne.us/business/bus_regist.html
City or County Business Licenses	Contact your city or county revenue department
Health Code Requirements and Permits	Contact your city or county health department
Small Business Administration Office	sba.gov/localresources/district/ne/index.html

Nevada

Nevada State Website	nv.gov
Information on Starting a Business	nv.gov/NV_default4.aspx?id=182
Business Structure Filing	nvsos.gov/index.aspx?page=415
Business Name Registration	File with County Clerk
Business Tax Registration	nevadatax.nv.gov/WEB/default.aspx
City or County Business Licenses	Contact your city or county revenue department
Health Code Requirements and Permits	Contact your city or county health department
Small Business Administration Office	sba.gov/localresources/district/nv/index.html

New Hampshire

New Hampshire State Website	nh.gov
Information on Starting a Business	nh.gov/business/
Business Structure Filing	http://www.sos.nh.gov/corporate/
Business Name Registration	sos.nh.gov/corporate/tradenameforms.html
Business Tax Registration	nh.gov/revenue/faq/gti-rev.htm
City or County Business Licenses	Contact your city or county revenue department
Health Code Requirements and Permits	Contact your city or county health department
Small Business Administration Office	sba.gov/localresources/district/nh/index.html

New Jersey

New Jersey State Website	state.nj.us
Information on Starting a Business	nj.gov/njbusiness/
Business Structure Filing	state.nj.us/treasury/revenue/dcr/filing/leadpg.htm
Business Name Registration	Register with County Clerk
Business Tax Registration	state.nj.us/treasury/revenue/dcr/filing/leadpg.htm
City or County Business Licenses	Contact your city or county revenue department
Health Code Requirements and Permits	Contact your city or county health department
Small Business Administration Office	sba.gov/localresources/district/nj/index.html

New Mexico

New Mexico State Website	newmexico.gov
Information on Starting a Business	newmexico.gov/business.php
Business Structure Filing	nmprc.state.nm.us/cb.htm
Business Name Registration	Not required in New Mexico
Business Tax Registration	tax.newmexico.gov/Businesses/Pages/Home.aspx
City or County Business Licenses	Contact your city or county revenue department
Health Code Requirements and Permits	Contact your city or county health department
Small Business Administration Office	sba.gov/localresources/district/nm/index.html

New York

New York State Website	state.ny.us
Information on Starting a Business	nysegov.com/citGuide.cfm?superCat=28
Business Structure Filing	nysegov.com/citGuide.cfm?superCat=28
Business Name Registration	Depends on business structure
Business Tax Registration	tax.state.ny.us/
City or County Business Licenses	Contact your city or county revenue department
Health Code Requirements and Permits	Contact your city or county health department
Small Business Administration Office	sba.gov/localresources/district/ny/

[140]

North Carolina
North Carolina State Website	ncgov.com
Information on Starting a Business	nccommerce.com/en/BusinessServices/StartYourBusiness/
Business Structure Filing	secretary.state.nc.us/corporations/
Business Name Registration	nccommerce.com/en/BusinessServices/StartYourBusiness/
Business Tax Registration	dornc.com/forms/index.html
City or County Business Licenses	Contact your city or county revenue department
Health Code Requirements and Permits	Contact your city or county health department
Small Business Administration Office	sba.gov/localresources/district/nc/index.html

North Dakota
North Dakota State Website	nd.gov
Information on Starting a Business	nd.gov/category.htm?id=69
Business Structure Filing	nd.gov/sos/businessserv
Business Name Registration	nd.gov/sos/businessserv/registrations/tradename.html
Business Tax Registration	nd.gov/businessreg
City or County Business Licenses	Contact your city or county revenue department
Health Code Requirements and Permits	Contact your city or county health department
Small Business Administration Office	sba.gov/localresources/district/nd/index.html

Ohio
Ohio State Website	ohio.gov
Information on Starting a Business	business.ohio.gov
Business Structure Filing	sos.state.oh.us/SOS/businessServices.aspx
Business Name Registration	sos.state.oh.us
Business Tax Registration	business.ohio.gov/efiling/
City or County Business Licenses	Contact your city or county revenue department
Health Code Requirements and Permits	Contact your city or county health department
Small Business Administration Office	sba.gov/localresources/district/oh/columbus/index.html

Oklahoma
Oklahoma State Website	ok.gov
Information on Starting a Business	ok.gov/section.php?sec_id=4
Business Structure Filing	sos.ok.gov/business/
Business Name Registration	sos.ok.gov/
Business Tax Registration	tax.ok.gov/
City or County Business Licenses	Contact your city or county revenue department
Health Code Requirements and Permits	Contact your city or county health department
Small Business Administration Office	sba.gov/localresources/district/ok/index.html

Oregon
Oregon State Website	oregon.gov
Information on Starting a Business	oregon.gov/menu_files/business_kut.shtml
Business Structure Filing	filinginoregon.com/business/index.htm
Business Name Registration	filinginoregon.com/business/
Business Tax Registration	oregon.gov/DOR/BUS/index.shtml
City or County Business Licenses	Contact your city or county revenue department
Health Code Requirements and Permits	Contact your city or county health department
Small Business Administration Office	sba.gov/localresources/district/or/index.html

Pennsylvania
Pennsylvania State Website	state.pa.us
Information on Starting a Business	pa.gov/portal/server.pt/community/work/3015
Business Structure Filing	dos.state.pa.us/portal/server.pt/community/corporation_bureau/12457
Business Name Registration	dos.state.pa.us/portal/server.pt/community/corporation_bureau/12457
Business Tax Registration	doreservices.state.pa.us/BusinessTax/PA100/FormatSelection.htm
City or County Business Licenses	Contact your city or county revenue department
Health Code Requirements and Permits	Contact your city or county health department
Small Business Administration Office	sba.gov/localresources/district/pa/

Puerto Rico

Puerto Rico State Website	topuertorico.org/government.shtml
Information on Starting a Business	gobierno.pr/G2B/Inicio/Inicio
Business Structure Filing	pr.gov/Estado/inicio/corporaciones.htm
Business Name Registration	pr.gov/Estado/inicio/marcas.htm
Business Tax Registration	hacienda.gobierno.pr/downloads/pdf/formularios /AS%202914.1.pdf
City or County Business Licenses	Contact your city or county revenue department
Health Code Requirements and Permits	Contact Department of Health for guidelines
Small Business Administration Office	sba.gov/localresources/district/pr/index.html

South Carolina

South Carolina State Website	sc.gov
Information on Starting a Business	sc.gov/business/Pages/default.aspx
Business Structure Filing	scsos.com/Business_Filings/Business _Filings_-_General_Information
Business Name Registration	Not required of domestic businesses
Business Tax Registration	scbos.sc.gov/
City or County Business Licenses	Contact your city or county revenue department
Health Code Requirements and Permits	Contact your city or county health department
Small Business Administration Office	sba.gov/localresources/district/sc/index.html

South Dakota

South Dakota State Website	sd.gov
Information on Starting a Business	sd.gov/servicedirect/
Business Structure Filing	sdsos.gov/busineservices/corporations.shtm
Business Name Registration	sdsos.gov/busineservices/fictitiousbusnames.shtm
Business Tax Registration	apps.sd.gov/applications/rv23cedar/main/main.aspx
City or County Business Licenses	Contact your city or county revenue department
Health Code Requirements and Permits	Contact your city or county health department
Small Business Administration Office	sba.gov/localresources/district/sd/index.html

Tennessee

Tennessee State Website	tennessee.gov
Information on Starting a Business	tennesseeanytime.org/business/index.html
Business Structure Filing	state.tn.us/sos/bus_svc/forms.htm
Business Name Registration	state.tn.us/sos/bus_svc/corporations.htm
Business Tax Registration	tennesseeanytime.org/bizreg/
City or County Business Licenses	Contact your city or county revenue department
Health Code Requirements and Permits	Contact your city or county health department
Small Business Administration Office	sba.gov/localresources/district/tn/index.html

Texas

Texas State Website	texas.gov
Information on Starting a Business	texas.gov/en/discover/Pages/topic.aspx ?topicid=%2Fbusiness%2Fstart
Business Structure Filing	Registration depends on business structure
Business Name Registration	Registration depends on business structure
Business Tax Registration	cpa.state.tx.us/taxpermit/
City or County Business Licenses	Contact your city or county revenue department
Health Code Requirements and Permits	Contact your city or county health department
Small Business Administration Office	sba.gov/localresources/district/tx/

US Virgin Islands

US Virgin Islands Website	ltg.gov.vi
Information on Starting a Business	dlca.vi.gov/
Business Structure Filing	ltg.gov.vi/corporations-and-trademarks.html
Business Name Registration	ltg.gov.vi/downloads/forms/ TRADENAMECERTIFICATE.pdf
Business Tax Registration	viirb.com/
City or County Business Licenses	Contact your local revenue department
Health Code Requirements and Permits	Contact Department of Health for guidelines

Utah

Utah State Website	utah.gov
Information on Starting a Business	business.utah.gov/
Business Structure Filing	corporations.utah.gov/
Business Name Registration	corporations.utah.gov/
Business Tax Registration	secure.utah.gov/osbr-user/user/welcome.html
City or County Business Licenses	Contact your city or county revenue department
Health Code Requirements and Permits	Contact your city or county health department
Small Business Administration Office	sba.gov/localresources/district/ut/index.html

Vermont

Vermont State Website	vermont.gov
Information on Starting a Business	vermont.gov/portal/business/
Business Structure Filing	sec.state.vt.us/corps/corpindex.htm
Business Name Registration	sec.state.vt.us/corps/forms/tradeapp.htm
Business Tax Registration	vermont.gov/portal/business/index.php?id=91
City or County Business Licenses	Contact your city or county revenue department
Health Code Requirements and Permits	Contact your city or county health department
Small Business Administration Office	sba.gov/localresources/district/vt/index.html

Virginia

Virginia State Website	virginia.gov
Information on Starting a Business	virginia.gov/cmsportal3/business_4096/
Business Structure Filing	scc.virginia.gov/clk/begin.aspx
Business Name Registration	Depends on business structure
Business Tax Registration	tax.virginia.gov/site.cfm?alias=BusinessHome
City or County Business Licenses	Contact your city or county revenue department
Health Code Requirements and Permits	Contact your city or county health department
Small Business Administration Office	sba.gov/localresources/district/va/index.html

Washington

Washington State Website	access.wa.gov
Information on Starting a Business	access.wa.gov/business/start.aspx
Business Structure Filing	sos.wa.gov/corps/Default.aspx
Business Name Registration	dol.wa.gov/business/faqtradename.html
Business Tax Registration	dor.wa.gov/content/doingbusiness/ registermybusiness/
City or County Business Licenses	Contact your city or county revenue department
Health Code Requirements and Permits	Contact your city or county health department
Small Business Administration Office	sba.gov/localresources/district/wa/index.html

West Virginia

West Virginia State Website	wv.gov
Information on Starting a Business	wv.gov/business/Pages/StartingaBusiness.aspx
Business Structure Filing	sos.wv.gov/Pages/default.aspx
Business Name Registration	sos.wv.gov/Pages/default.aspx
Business Tax Registration	wva.state.wv.us/wvtax/default.aspx
City or County Business Licenses	Contact your city or county revenue department
Health Code Requirements and Permits	Contact your city or county health department
Small Business Administration Office	sba.gov/localresources/district/wv/index.html

Wisconsin

Wisconsin State Website	wisconsin.gov
Information on Starting a Business	wisconsin.gov/state/core/business.html
Business Structure Filing	wdfi.org/corporations/forms/
Business Name Registration	wisconsin.gov/state/byb/name.html
Business Tax Registration	revenue.wi.gov/faqs/pcs/btr-on.html
City or County Business Licenses	Contact your city or county revenue department
Health Code Requirements and Permits	Contact your city or county health department
Small Business Administration Office	sba.gov/localresources/district/wi/index.html

Wyoming

Wyoming State Website	wyoming.gov
Information on Starting a Business	wyomingbusiness.org/business/txt_starting.htm
Business Structure Filing	soswy.state.wy.us/Forms/FormsFiling.aspx ?startwith=Business
Business Name Registration	soswy.state.wy.us/Forms/FormsFiling.aspx ?startwith=Business
Business Tax Registration	revenue.state.wy.us/PortalVBVS/ DesktopDefault.aspx?tabindex=2&tabid=9
City or County Business Licenses	Contact your city or county revenue department
Health Code Requirements and Permits	Contact your city or county health department
Small Business Administration Office	sba.gov/localresources/district/wy/index.html

ACKNOWLEDGEMENTS

There are so many people I am deeply indebted to for this book I don't know where to start. Since she says she's always the last to hear anything, I owe my sister, Joanna Lewis, the first thank you in this book. She runs one of the most beautiful retail stores in Jackson Hole Wyoming so if you're ever there be sure to stop into Ella's Room to see a true visionary small businesswoman at work.

My parents, Jim and Jean Lewis, didn't blink an eye when I told them I was thinking about transitioning out of the culinary world and going to business school instead. They also did multiple reads of various drafts of this book to make sure that all the facts are correct, my numbers add up, and that everything makes sense. Throughout my life they have always encouraged me to "reach for the cookies" in everything I pursue.

Bryan Jaffe is one of the most brilliant business minds I have ever met. He is also, luckily for me, my beloved husband. He has been my rock through every minute of the business building process from writing the business plan to helping me make strategic decisions about Petit Four Legs. He also helped me rework sections of this book so that everything is clearly worded and inline with common business practices.

Like food, a good book must be visually appealing and for that I thank Michelle Draeger of mdraeger design. Her cover art exceeded all expectations and clearly captures the opportunity that is available to part-time food entrepreneurs.

I also need to thank the entrepreneurs mentioned in this book; Rhienn Davis of Cakes by Look, Kristina Bavik, former co-founder of Svedela Bakery, Aaron Barthel of Intrigue Chocolates Co., Matt Pierce of Primal Pacs, Cle Franklin of Half Pint Ice Cream, and Marcia Newlands, former owner of The Savory Gourmet. The craftsmanship of their products is a testament to the fact that the small business spirit and focus on high-quality goods is alive and well. If you ever have a chance, be sure to taste their products. You will not be disappointed.

I was fortunate enough to meet Zoe Bartlett during the founding years of her own food business. I am grateful for her friendship, energy and unflagging enthusiasm and can't wait to see the next adventure she creates for herself.

Ashley Yotsuuye was the first non-editor to read this book and her candid feedback and suggestions have only strengthened the book.

I am grateful to the professors at the Kellogg School of Management at Northwestern University who were able to turn a pastry chef into a businesswoman which is no simple task. It was there that I also made lasting friendships with incredible people who are doing amazing things in the world today.

Lastly, I want to thank Greta and Tyr for making sure no matter how bogged down with work I get I always make time to go for a walk.

61874680R00084

Made in the USA
Middletown, DE
15 January 2018